AQA GCSE
ENGLISH AND ENGLISH LANGUAGE

UNIT 1 HIGHER TIER

Beverley Emm

CONSULTANT: DAVID STONE

OXFORD
UNIVERSITY PRESS

Contents

Introduction

What is in your Unit 1 exam?

If you are following the AQA GCSE course in English or English Language, you will be sitting the Unit 1 exam. Unit 1 focuses on communication between reader and writer, and deals specifically with non-fiction texts, those that are based on real life. The exam tests your ability to understand and produce non-fiction texts, which means that at different stages you are both the reader and the writer. The exam is worth 40% of your total GCSE marks. It lasts 2 hours 15 minutes and is marked out of 80.

There are two sections in the exam:

- Section A: Reading. This is worth 40 marks. It is where you are the reader and your ability to understand a range of non-fiction texts is assessed. You have to answer four questions based on three reading sources.

- Section B: Writing. This is worth 40 marks. It is where you are the writer and your ability to produce non-fiction texts is assessed. You have to complete two writing tasks: one shorter task worth 16 marks and one longer task worth 24 marks.

How to use this book

There are six questions in the Unit 1H exam and you are expected to demonstrate different skills in each one. This book is therefore divided into six chapters, with each one focusing on a separate question. It starts with Question 1 and ends with Question 6, but it is not essential to work through the chapters in order.

Each chapter shows you how to approach the question in the exam and the key skills you need to demonstrate when writing your response. In each chapter you will find:

- a range of texts similar to those you will encounter in the exam

- an extract from the Mark Scheme that examiners use to mark your response, so that you can see exactly what skills are being assessed in each question

- sample questions with the key skills identified

- advice on how to demonstrate and combine the key skills in your response

- individual, pair and small-group activities to practise and reinforce the key skills

- sample student responses

- opportunities for self-assessment and peer-assessment

- advice on how to improve your responses.

Preparing for Section A: Reading

What is the content and focus of the exam?

Unit 1 Section A is worth 40 marks. It is where you are the reader and your ability to understand a range of non-fiction texts is assessed. You have to answer four questions based on three reading sources. These sources may be functional, such as information leaflets, or they may be texts you would read in everyday life, such as media sources and literary non-fiction, for example, travelogues and biographies. The sources may be linked by a theme.

How to use your time in the exam

You should aim to spend 1 hour 15 minutes on the Reading section (leaving 1 hour for the Writing section). The following provides a suggestion for how you could divide up your time in the Reading section of the exam:

Question and approach	Marks available	Suggested timing
Question 1: Read Source 1 then answer Question 1 (while the information is still fresh in your mind).	8 marks	15 minutes
Question 2: Read Source 2 then answer Question 2.	8 marks	15 minutes
Question 3: Read Source 3 then answer Question 3.	8 marks	15 minutes
Question 4: Answer Question 4 (there are no new source texts for this question).	16 marks	30 minutes

Each of the four questions is testing a different skill. This Reading section is therefore divided into four chapters, with each one focusing on a separate question. It is essential that you attempt all four Reading questions in the exam in order to demonstrate all the necessary skills. If you miss out a question, you will not achieve the mark that you want.

Assessment Objectives (AOs)

Assessment Objectives are the skills being assessed during your GCSE course. Below is a table that shows you the AOs that you need to demonstrate in the Reading section of the Unit 1 exam:

AO number	AO wording	Question this AO applies to in Section A: Reading
AO2, i English AO3, i English Language	Read and understand texts, selecting material appropriate to purpose, collating from different sources and making comparisons and cross-references as appropriate.	You need to demonstrate this AO in Question 1, Question 3 and Question 4.
AO2, iii English AO3, iii English Language	Explain and evaluate how writers use linguistic, grammatical, structural and presentational features to achieve effects and engage and influence the reader.	You need to demonstrate this AO in Question 2 and Question 4.

By working through the Reading chapters of this book, you will practise these key skills and learn exactly where you need to demonstrate them in the exam in order to achieve your best possible mark.

Mark Scheme

Imagine a ladder with four rungs. Each rung represents a band in a Mark Scheme. The examiner uses this Mark Scheme to assess your responses: the bottom rung is Band 1 and the top rung is Band 4.

Each mark band is summed up by a key word or words. For Reading, the key words are:

Band 4: perceptive/detailed
Band 3: clear/relevant
Band 2: some/attempts
Band 1: limited

Each mark band consists of a range of skills, based on the Assessment Objectives above, which students have to demonstrate – the further up the ladder you climb, the more demanding the skills become. Although the key words are common throughout the Reading section, the skills being tested in each question are different, so an extract from the Mark Scheme that examiners use for each question is included at the beginning of each chapter.

Higher tier students are aiming for Band 3 or Band 4 and this book aims to help you achieve the best mark of which you are capable.

Practising the key skills

What to expect in the exam

In the exam, Question 1 is based on Source 1 and is worth 8 marks. You are asked to do three things in your response. These are summarized in the annotations around the sample question below.

*You are being asked to **retrieve** the important information and ideas in an article. To retrieve something means to find it in the text.*

*You are being asked to **support** the important information and ideas that you retrieve. To support something means to back up what you say with evidence from the text.*

*You are being asked to **interpret** the important information and ideas that you retrieve. To interpret something means to read 'between the lines'. It's what you can work out from the text without actually being told. To show that you understand the article, you are expected to do more than just retrieve.*

What do you understand from the article about ...?

The rest of the question will depend on what the article is about.

An extract from the Mark Scheme that examiners use to mark Question 1 is printed below. There are four mark bands in total, but Higher tier students are aiming for Band 3 or Band 4. The key words for each band are on the left-hand side and the skills you have to demonstrate in your response are on the right. Notice the differences between Band 3 and Band 4.

Exam tips

- To achieve Band 4, you need to discuss all aspects of the issue or issues in detail.

- If there is a picture in the article, you should not comment on it. It is just there to help your understanding of the text.

- You should not comment on the use of language for this question. Comments on the use of language do not gain you any marks in Question 1.

AO2, i English AO3, i English Language	Skills
Band 4 'perceptive' 'detailed' 7–8 marks	• offers evidence that the text is fully understood • shows a detailed engagement with the text • makes perceptive connections and comments • offers appropriate quotations or references to support understanding
Band 3 'clear' 'relevant' 5–6 marks	• shows clear evidence that the text is understood • shows clear engagement with the text • begins to interpret the text and make connections • offers relevant quotations or references to support understanding

Retrieving information and ideas

First, look at how to retrieve the important information and ideas. To retrieve something means to find it in the text. You are looking for the important information and ideas in a text to show that you understand what the writer is saying.

Read the following extract, 'Facebook generation suffer information withdrawal syndrome' by Richard Gray. It is taken from an article about a recent experiment to see how young people cope when modern technology is taken away from them.

Facebook generation suffer information withdrawal syndrome

Scientists asked volunteers to stay away from all emails, text messages, Facebook and Twitter updates for 24 hours. They found that the participants began to develop symptoms typically seen in smokers attempting to give up. Some of those taking part said they felt like they were undergoing 'cold turkey' to break a hard drug habit, while others said it felt like going on a diet. The condition is now being described as Information Deprivation Disorder.

Dr Roman Gerodimos, a lecturer in communication who led the UK section of the international study, said: 'We were not just seeing psychological symptoms, but also physical symptoms. Some people didn't find it hard, while a minority hated it. The majority struggled at first, experiencing these symptoms, before they developed coping mechanisms that helped to distract them.'

The findings will fuel concerns raised by neurologists and

psychologists about the impact that excessive use of the Internet, computer games and social networking sites are having on the so-called 'Net Generation' of teenagers and young adults.

Activity 1

1. Identify the important information and ideas in the extract by making a list of five key points. One example might be: 'Some volunteers said giving up technology for 24 hours was like trying to come off drugs.'

2. Discuss your key points with a partner to see if you have found the most important information and ideas in the extract.

Exam tips

It is a good idea to work your way through the text in the order in which things happen so that you can discuss the writer's argument in a logical way.

One way to do this is to imagine the writer had a plan with key points that he wanted to include in his article. What would his plan be?

Supporting the information and ideas

Now look at how to support the important information and ideas that you retrieve. To support something means to back up what you say with evidence from the text. You need to select actual words and phrases from the text to show where your understanding has come from.

Activity 2

1. Select words and phrases from the text on page 7 to back up the important information and ideas you retrieved.

2. By the side of each key point, copy your selected words or phrases. One example for the key point given in Activity 1 might be: 'They felt like they were undergoing "cold turkey" to break a hard drug habit.'

3. Discuss your selection with a partner to see if you have found the best words and phrases to support the key points that you retrieved.

Exam tips

To interpret also means to infer meaning from a text; to comment on parts of a text using your own words; to make connections between parts of a text; and to deduce.

Interpreting the information and ideas

Now look at how to interpret the important information and ideas that you retrieve. To interpret something means to read 'between the lines'. It's working out what the text is saying, without actually being told explicitly. To show that you understand the article, you are expected to do more than just retrieve. You should comment on the important information and ideas in order to show that you understand what the writer might be suggesting.

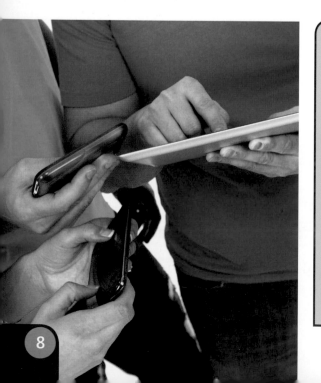

Activity 3

1. Read 'between the lines' of the extract to work out what the writer might be suggesting from the important information and ideas that you retrieved.

2. Draw up a table like the one opposite. Add your five key points to the column headed 'Retrieval' and your supporting words and phrases in the column headed 'Support'.

3. Add your comments on what you think the writer might be suggesting in the column headed 'Interpretation'. Two examples have been done for you.

4. Discuss your table with a partner to see if you have interpreted the key points in an effective way.

Retrieval	Support	Interpretation
1.		
2. Some volunteers said giving up technology for 24 hours was like trying to come off drugs.	'They felt like they were undergoing "cold turkey" to break a hard drug habit.'	This suggests that things like texting and Facebook are extremely addictive.
3.		
4.		
5. Doctors are worried about the impact of using the Internet too much.	'The findings will fuel concerns raised by neurologists and psychologists.'	This suggests the study has increased doctors' fears about the harmful effects of the Internet on young people.

Exam tips

- Notice the phrase 'This suggests that…'. This shows the examiner that you are beginning to interpret, which is a Band 3 skill. Other useful phrases include: 'This means…', 'This lets us know…', 'This indicates…', 'This implies…' and 'This makes me think…'.

- It is worth noting that if you were to write up the points from your table in continuous prose, they would form a whole response.

Combining key skills

Now look at another article, and combine the key skills of retrieving, supporting and interpreting.

Read the following extract, 'IQ tests: women score higher than men' by Harriet Cooke. It is taken from an article about how men and women perform in intelligence tests.

IQ tests: women score higher than men

Women have scored higher than men in intelligence testing for the first time since records began. The findings represent a dramatic twist in the battle of the sexes, as in the past 100 years of IQ testing, women have lagged behind men by as much as five points.

But now the gap has closed and females have stolen the lead.

The results have been published by James Flynn, a world-renowned expert in

IQ testing, who believes the demands of the modern age are raising standards of intelligence. He said: 'In the last 100 years the IQ scores of both men and women have risen, but women's

have risen faster. This is a consequence of modernity. The complexity of the modern world is making our brains adapt and raising our IQ.'

One theory for the result is that the demands of juggling family life and building a career have made women more intelligent. Another theory is those women have always had the potential for higher results, but are only now realizing it.

Activity 4

1. Make a table like the one on page 9 with three columns headed 'Retrieval', 'Support' and 'Interpretation'. Then see if you can fill it in, with the important information and ideas in the left-hand column, some supporting words and phrases in the middle column and some comments to show what the writer might be suggesting in the right-hand column.

2. Discuss your table with a partner to see if you retrieved the most important information and ideas, selected the best words and phrases to support, and interpreted the key points in an effective way.

Now read the following sample taken from Student A's response to the article, 'IQ tests: women score higher than men'. It is annotated to show how the key skills of retrieving, supporting and interpreting can be combined. This sample would be placed in Band 3.

> What do you understand from the article about men's and women's performance in IQ tests?

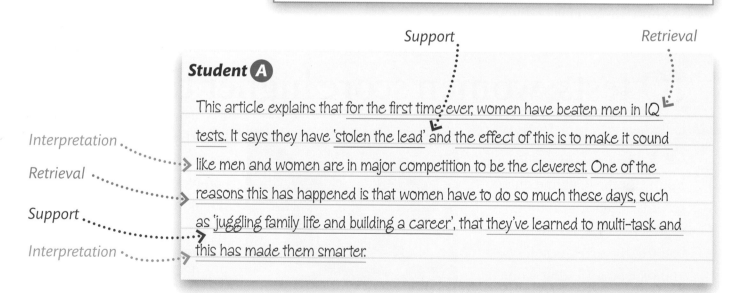

Support   *Retrieval*

Student A

This article explains that for the first time ever, women have beaten men in IQ tests. It says they have 'stolen the lead' and the effect of this is to make it sound like men and women are in major competition to be the cleverest. One of the reasons this has happened is that women have to do so much these days, such as 'juggling family life and building a career', that they've learned to multi-task and this has made them smarter.

Interpretation
Retrieval
Support
Interpretation

Now read a sample taken from Student B's response. It would be placed in Band 4.

Student B

This article explains how levels of intelligence have risen in both men and women over the last 100 years but for the first time, women are scoring higher in IQ tests and there are a number of theories why this has happened. One idea is that people's brains have adapted due to the 'consequence of modernity', meaning society puts more pressure on people than it did in the past, especially women as traditional male roles have become less defined and women take on more. It says 'the demands of juggling family life and building a career have made women more intelligent', suggesting the more work and responsibility you have in life, the smarter you become. However, it also states that 'women have always had the potential for higher results', so it may not actually be a recent change in their intelligence, rather they are 'only now realizing it'.

Activity 5

1. Copy out Student B's answer and highlight all the words that show the important information and ideas that have been retrieved.

2. In a second colour, highlight all the supporting words and phrases taken from the text.

3. In a third colour, highlight all the comments that show interpretation.

4. Discuss your highlighted response with a partner to see if you agree.

Exam tips

- It is a good idea to start your response with an overview sentence to show you have a grasp of the whole argument before going into detail.

- Look at both the choice of words and phrases used to support and also how they have been used in the response.

Activity 6

In groups of four, re-read the two student samples and discuss what Student B does that Student A doesn't. To get you started, you could compare:

1. the opening sentences

2. the selection of important information and ideas that has been retrieved

3. how the text has been used to support

4. the sort of comments made to interpret.

Try it yourself (with support)

Writing your own complete response

Now you are going to practise using all the key skills in a complete response to Question 1. You'll be given some support to help you do this.

Look back over pages 6–11 to remind yourself of how to approach Question 1, then read the article below, 'Panda breeding success ignores their disappearing habitat' by Wang Dajun. This is similar in length to the source you will have in the exam.

Panda breeding success ignores their disappearing habitat

By Wang Dajun

IMAGES OF A DOZEN or more baby pandas being shown off to the public by researchers or reserve staff is a common sight in the media these days, giving the impression that giant-panda conservation is flourishing. This is misleading: captive breeding may have proved successful, but it's no substitute for protecting wild populations and their habitats. Here, there is little cause for celebration.

In 2007, a captive-bred male panda named Xiang Xiang was returned to the wild by Wulong Panda Research Centre, but did not survive – he is thought to have fallen from a tree after being chased by other pandas. Subsequent research indicates new female arrivals are more readily accepted by wild populations than males. If that had been known earlier, the experiment may have been more successful.

The research centre has since been more cautious about returning pandas to the wild. A panda called Caocao and her cub are gradually being moved from a low-altitude training ground to higher-altitude locations. In April last year, the centre told the media that efforts to train pandas to be returned to the wild would expand.

These experiments have benefits for both scientific knowledge and the management of panda populations. But returning pandas to the wild does not solve the real thorn in the side of panda conservation. The main and urgent problem that wild panda populations face is the destruction and break-up of their habitat: if good habitats are available, the populations will grow naturally and there will be no need to introduce new individuals. Without high quality habitats, however, no matter how many pandas we raise in captivity, there will be nowhere to put them.

There is another worry. The successful artificial breeding and rearing of pandas at Wulong and at the Chengdu Panda Breeding Centre has become a model for others, and there are aspirations for more breeding centres and more baby pandas to demonstrate the successes of conservation. Such a proliferation of centres may lead to animals actually being taken from the wild to supply them – in fact, this is already happening. And it will have the same effect on wild populations as poaching.

The panda has unique cultural and diplomatic significance for China. But, today, too much attention is paid to captive breeding programmes, and conservation in the wild has been demoted. This is a mistake.

The experience of the last 20 years has taught us that conservation is not just about protecting a species – it is also about protecting the environment in which we live. How do you measure 'success' in protecting a species? I say by the conservation and restoration of both the animal and its habitat.

Activity 7

What do you understand from the article about the issues of panda conservation?

Remember to:

- start with an overview sentence to show that you have a grasp of the whole argument
- retrieve the important information and ideas in the text
- support the important information and ideas with words and phrases from the text
- read 'between the lines' to work out what the writer might be suggesting.

Peer-assessment

Activity 8

1. Now swap your response with a partner. Does your partner's response:

   a. start with an overview sentence to show there is a grasp of the whole argument?

   b. retrieve the important information and ideas in the text?

   c. discuss all aspects of the issue or issues in detail?

   d. support the important information and ideas with words and phrases from the text?

   e. read 'between the lines' to work out what the writer might be suggesting?

2. Make some notes on what your partner has done successfully and what could be improved.

3. Now spend a few minutes giving your partner some feedback on their work.

Improving your answer

Now read the following example of a complete response to 'Panda breeding success ignores their disappearing habitat' on page 14. As it stands, it would be placed in Band 3, but the annotations show how you could improve the response by developing parts of it further. This would move it up into Band 4. You would not need to include all of these additions to move into Band 4; they are just examples of the sort of things you could say.

Exam tips

- Remember, you are aiming to discuss all aspects of the issue or issues in detail.
- You should not include any additional information in your response. Everything you say should come from the text.
- Remember, you should not comment on the picture in your response.
- Remember, you should not comment on the use of language for this question.

> ## What do you understand from the article about the issues of panda conservation?

To move into Band 4, you could add: '... although this success, in itself, has created other problems for China'.

To move into Band 4, you could add: 'This suggests that there are very few suitable habitats left in China for pandas to live in as, if there were, pandas would breed and expand their population naturally.'

To move into Band 4, you could add: 'Another problem connected to this is that because the "artificial breeding and rearing" is so successful, people are taking pandas out of the wild to put into the conservation centres, which is reducing the natural panda population rather than having the opposite, desired effect of increasing it. The writer says this has "the same effect as poaching".'

The article explains that panda conservation looks like it is working because China has set up lots of panda research centres and it mentions 'the successful artificial breeding and rearing of pandas at Wulong'. However, I now understand this may be 'misleading' because the writer believes not enough is being done to protect 'wild populations and their habitats', plus it is also really hard to put captive-bred pandas back into the wild.

One panda called Xiang Xiang was returned by Wulong but he was 'thought to have fallen from a tree after being chased by other pandas' and was killed. This suggests that pandas bred in captivity aren't always accepted by the naturally wild pandas that are already there. Since then, scientists have discovered that 'new female arrivals are more readily accepted by wild populations than males' so they are preparing a female panda called Caocao and her cub to be returned. This should mean they have a better chance of the experiment working this time.

One of the big problems I understand from this article is that people are destroying the places where pandas live. The writer says 'the main and urgent problem that wild panda populations face is the destruction and break-up of their habitat'. He says it doesn't matter how good they are at breeding and rearing giant pandas in captivity if there is nowhere for them to go afterwards.

China obviously wants to keep its panda population because 'the panda has unique cultural and diplomatic significance for China', but at the moment the writer thinks they're not really going about it the right way.

To move into Band 4, you could add: 'He thinks too much attention has been placed on captive breeding programmes at the expense of conservation in the wild and says the only way to ensure a species is protected is by "the conservation and restoration of both the animal and its habitat".'

Peer-assessment

Activity 9

Having looked at the student response opposite, which shows you how to move a Band 3 response up to Band 4, complete the following tasks:

1. Look again at your own response to 'Panda breeding success ignores their disappearing habitat'. With your partner, decide which band your response fits into at the moment. Use the Mark Scheme on page 6 to help you make your decision.

2. Discuss which parts of your response you could develop in order to improve it.

3. Rewrite your response with the parts you developed, and see if you have now achieved a higher mark.

So far, you have learnt how to approach Question 1 by focusing on three key skills:

● retrieving

● supporting

● interpreting.

Now see how confident you feel that you have understood this approach by completing the self-assessment below.

Self-assessment

1.	I have learnt that I need to retrieve the important information and ideas from the text.	Not sure	Confident
2.	I have learnt that I need to support what I retrieve with words and phrases from the text.	Not sure	Confident
3.	I have learnt that I need to interpret what the writer might be suggesting in the text.	Not sure	Confident
4.	I have learnt that it is a good idea to start with an overview sentence to show that I have a grasp of the whole argument.	Not sure	Confident
5.	I have learnt that I have to discuss all aspects of the issue or issues in detail.	Not sure	Confident
6.	I have learnt that I should not comment on the use of language for this question.	Not sure	Confident

Try it yourself (on your own)

Finally, read the article opposite, 'Dogs in the classroom: reading with a fluffy friend' by Clover Stroud and write your own complete response to the sample Question 1 task in Activity 10, applying all the key skills you have learnt.

Read the Mark Scheme below before you complete Activity 10. The Mark Scheme will help you to remember what is being assessed.

AO2, i English AO3, i English Language	Skills
Band 4 'perceptive' 'detailed' 7–8 marks	• offers evidence that the text is fully understood • shows a detailed engagement with the text • makes perceptive connections and comments • offers appropriate quotations or references to support understanding
Band 3 'clear' 'relevant' 5–6 marks	• shows clear evidence that the text is understood • shows clear engagement with the text • begins to interpret the text and make connections • offers relevant quotations or references to support understanding

Activity 10

Complete the following sample Question 1 task using the article opposite.

> What do you understand from the article about the Dogs Helping Kids programme set up by Tracey Berridge?

Dogs in the classroom: reading with a fluffy friend

By Clover Stroud

At a primary school in Devon, a class of eight-year-olds is finishing a literacy exercise. It's a scene familiar to hundreds of classrooms, except that lying quietly in one corner is Wynona, an Alaskan malamute.

Wynona was trained by Tracey Berridge, a canine behaviourist trainer, who set up Dogs Helping Kids in 2003 to take dogs into classrooms, both as therapeutic aids for teaching children about kindness and empathy, and also for providing reading support.

Stretched out on her blanket, Wynona's calming presence is almost tangible as the children work near her, occasionally looking up to smile at their canine classroom assistant, before returning to their writing.

Inspired by a documentary she saw as a teenager about the positive influence of dogs on education, Tracey, 41, is dedicated to taking dogs into schools. It's a timely move. National literacy is under scrutiny, with figures suggesting one in six pupils struggle to read fluently by the age of 11. Nick Gibb, the Schools Minister, has said existing targets and reading lists are too 'modest'.

Tracey is hoping to help as many children as possible reach more ambitious literacy goals with her dogs. Her work is voluntary, as is the assistance of the owners, and although she's based in Devon, she's also training dogs in Wales, Lincoln and Stafford.

Tracey has worked in nearly 50 schools, and with library reading groups, but started the charity after being invited by a teenage behavioural unit to take her own dog, a lurcher cross called Princess Laya, to work with violent adolescents. 'Spending time with Laya improved self-esteem and confidence, which had a remarkable effect on behaviour. It inspired me to continue, even though people thought I was loony when I talked about taking dogs into schools in the Nineties.'

And because children love seeing the dogs, their presence has helped cut truancy. Doug Campbell, deputy head of Forches Cross Primary School in Barnstaple, has witnessed a change in his pupils since Berridge started bringing in Wynona: 'We're in an area with high social and educational needs, and attendance is a problem. The calming effect of Wynona is encouraging, as she seems to motivate and incentivize.'

The 'listening canines' are trained to focus on a book a child is reading, and children are told they are teaching the dog to read. 'The children feel in control, and it makes reading fun again.'

Back in the classroom, Wynona waits for a signal that the lesson is over. The children all want to know when she will be back. 'They feel they have a really supportive ally with them,' says Tracey.

Practising the key skills

What to expect in the exam

In the exam, Question 2 is based on Source 2 and is worth 8 marks. You are asked to do four things in your response. These are summarized in the annotations around the sample question below.

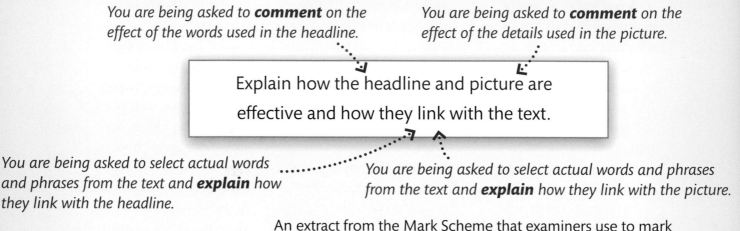

*You are being asked to **comment** on the effect of the words used in the headline.*

*You are being asked to **comment** on the effect of the details used in the picture.*

Explain how the headline and picture are effective and how they link with the text.

*You are being asked to select actual words and phrases from the text and **explain** how they link with the headline.*

*You are being asked to select actual words and phrases from the text and **explain** how they link with the picture.*

An extract from the Mark Scheme that examiners use to mark Question 2 is printed below. There are four mark bands in total, but Higher tier students are aiming for Band 3 or Band 4. The key words for each band are on the left-hand side and the skills you have to demonstrate in your response are on the right. Notice the differences between Band 3 and Band 4.

Exam tips

- To achieve Band 4, both the headline and the picture need to be discussed. You should also aim to discuss both for Band 3.

- You are not being asked to link the headline and picture together.

AO2, iii English AO3, iii English Language	Skills
Band 4 'perceptive' 'detailed' 7–8 marks	• offers a detailed interpretation of the effects of the headline • presents a detailed explanation and interpretation of what the picture shows and its effect • links the picture and the headline to the text with perceptive comments • offers appropriate quotations or references to support comments
Band 3 'clear' 'relevant' 5–6 marks	• shows clear evidence that the headline and its effects are understood • makes clear and appropriate links between the headline and the content of the text • offers a clear explanation of the effectiveness of the picture • links the picture to the content of the text • employs relevant quotations or references

Looking at headlines

First, look at the effect of the words used in a headline. The example below is from an article about some local rail enthusiasts in Yorkshire. Their plans to re-open a disused railway as a tourist attraction have been approved.

Full steam ahead for railway plans

Activity 1

1. Why has the writer chosen to use these particular words?

2. What effect is the writer trying to create?

3. Think about these words in relation to what you know about this article. How do they add to your understanding of what is happening?

Below is a sample taken from a Band 3 response, with annotations to show why it would be placed in this mark band.

This identifies a technique the writer has used in the headline.

This selects actual words from the headline.

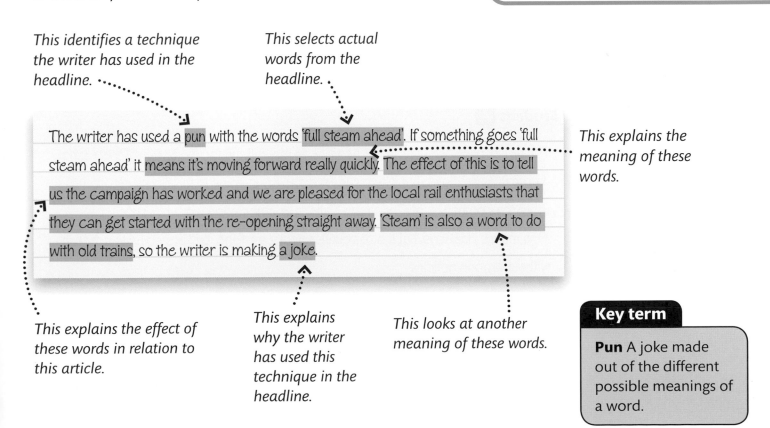

The writer has used a pun with the words 'full steam ahead'. If something goes 'full steam ahead' it means it's moving forward really quickly. The effect of this is to tell us the campaign has worked and we are pleased for the local rail enthusiasts that they can get started with the re-opening straight away. 'Steam' is also a word to do with old trains, so the writer is making a joke.

This explains the meaning of these words.

This explains the effect of these words in relation to this article.

This explains why the writer has used this technique in the headline.

This looks at another meaning of these words.

Key term

Pun A joke made out of the different possible meanings of a word.

Looking at another headline

The headline below is from an article about a range of toy crabs. They have been a huge hit with children in America and are due to be launched in the UK in time for Christmas.

Crawling crabs sidle into UK to pinch festive sales

Exam tips

In the exam, there are lots of other features you can look out for as well as puns.

Key term

Alliteration The deliberate repetition of the same sound at the beginning of words to create an effect, e.g. 'crawling crabs'.

Activity 2

1. The word 'pinch' is one example of a pun. See if you can find another example.

2. Explain the different possible meanings of these words.

3. Think about these words in relation to what you know about this article. How do they add to your understanding of what is happening?

4. The writer also uses **alliteration** in the headline. What effect does this add?

Read the following two student samples. Student A's is taken from a Band 3 response and Student B's is taken from a Band 4 response.

Student A

The writer uses two puns in the headline to make it fun for the reader. 'Pinch' is how a crab uses its claws, but it also suggests the toy is going to steal business from other toy companies at Christmas. 'Sidle' is another good word because a real crab moves sideways, but it also sounds sneaky, as if the toys are going to creep in without anyone noticing.

Student B

The writer uses two puns in this headline, partly to make it fun for the reader but also to hint at something more devious. 'Sidle' is used to represent the sideways movement of a crab, but it also suggests the almost unnoticeable movement of the toys as they enter the UK. It's like they're creeping in and sneakily taking over the Christmas toy market. This is reinforced by 'pinch', which is less subtle than 'sidle' and is a quick, sharp word. As well as indicating the characteristics of a crab, it implies the toys are powerful and are confidently going to steal all the sales at the shops.

Activity 3

In groups of four, re-read the two student samples and discuss what Student B does that Student A doesn't. To get you started, you could compare:

1. the opening sentences

2. the sort of comments made about the effects.

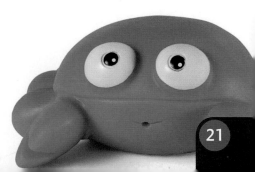

21

Linking the headline with the text

Next, you have to think about linking the headline with the content of the text.

This is an extract from the original 'crawling crabs' article:

A toy crab which has taken the US by storm is being launched in the UK in time for Christmas, the toy distributor Character said yesterday. The range of four crawling crabs, which have 12 changeable shells and come with an extra mini-toy, were due for release in the New Year, but the launch has been brought forward to the second week of December following success in the US, where one is sold every seven seconds. The group said sales rose 11 per cent to £95m in the year to 31 August, while pre-tax profits gained 20 per cent to £9.1m.

In your response to Question 2, you need to select actual words and phrases from the text of the article to show the links between the headline and the text.

Now read Student A's sample opposite, which is taken from a Band 3 response. This is an example of how you could make links between the words in the headline (see page 20) and the text of the 'crawling crabs' article above. The highlighted words are the links that help to explain how this is an effective headline for this article.

Student Ⓐ

The writer uses two puns in the headline to make it fun for the reader. 'Pinch' is how a crab uses its claws, but it also suggests the toy is going to steal business from other toy companies at Christmas. The text says that one is sold 'every seven seconds' in America, which means it's really popular and will probably be a huge hit in the UK as well. 'Sidle' is another good word because a real crab moves sideways, but it also sounds sneaky, as if the toys are going to creep in without anyone noticing, especially as the launch has been 'brought forward to the second week of December'.

Activity 4
· ·

Re-read Student B's sample below, taken from a Band 4 response.

1. Using Student B's sample, choose some words and phrases from the original 'crawling crabs' article on the opposite page that show the links between the headline and the text.

2. Copy out Student B's sample and include your chosen words and phrases to make links between the words in the headline and the text of the 'crawling crabs' article.

3. Discuss your final response with a partner to see how successful you have been. To get you started, explain how your chosen words and phrases show why the headline is effective for this text.

Student Ⓑ

The writer uses two puns in this headline, partly to make it fun for the reader but also to hint at something more devious. 'Sidle' is used to represent the sideways movement of a crab, but it also suggests the almost unnoticeable movement of the toys as they enter the UK. It's like they're creeping in and sneakily taking over the Christmas toy market. This is reinforced by 'pinch', which is less subtle than 'sidle' and is a quick, sharp word. As well as indicating the characteristics of a crab, it implies the toys have power and are confidently going to steal all the sales at the shops.

Exam tips

The use of scale and colour in a picture is often worth mentioning, and camera angles can also be important. Also, try to consider the less obvious details, such as a person's facial expression or what is happening in the background.

Looking at pictures

Next, look at the effect of the details used in a picture.

The picture below is from an article about a street theatre company that visited Liverpool on the anniversary of the sinking of the *Titanic*. There were three giant puppets and this one is called Little Girl.

Activity 5

1. List six details in this picture. To get you started, the puppet's strings are attached to a huge crane.

2. Explain why the writer has chosen a picture with these particular details.

3. What effect is the writer trying to create?

4. Think about these details in relation to what you know about this article. How do they add to your understanding of what is happening?

Read the following sample. This is taken from a Band 3 response, with annotations so that you can see why it would be placed in this band.

This gives the context of the picture.　　　*This identifies actual details in the picture.*

The picture shows Little Girl, one of the three giant puppets that was part of the street theatre company visiting Liverpool. We can see the huge crane holding her strings and the people watching in the background look tiny to emphasize how big the puppet is. There is also a real little girl staring up at her who looks extremely small and the effect of this is to reinforce the scale and show that Little Girl really isn't little at all!

This explains the importance of these details.　　　*This explains the effect of these details in relation to the article.*

Looking at another picture

Now look at the effect of the details used in another picture (below) which is from an article about the challenges of raising an exceptionally gifted child.

Exam tips

Sometimes students say 'this is effective because it attracts the reader' or 'this is effective because it makes it stand out', but these comments are too general. They could apply to any picture. The effects of the details you select need to be connected to the article you're reading.

Activity 6

1. List six details in this picture. To get you started, the boy has drawn a penguin on the blackboard.

2. Explain why the writer has chosen a picture with these particular details.

3. What effect is the writer trying to create?

4. Think about these details in relation to what you know about this article. How do they add to your understanding of what is happening?

Read the following two student samples. Student A's is taken from a Band 3 response and Student B's is from a Band 4 response.

Student A

In the picture, the young boy has drawn lots of squiggles and a penguin, which is typical of a small child. However, he has also written an equation which shows that although he is young, he is gifted and sometimes his mental age is greater than his real age.

Student B

In the picture, the young boy has drawn lots of squiggles and a penguin, and he is standing next to a giant cuddly toy, all of which is typical of young children and represents his innocence. However, this contrasts with the complex mathematical equation written on the board as it is something way beyond his age. From this, we can see two very different sides to this boy. Physically, and maybe emotionally, he is still very young, but mentally he can understand much more complicated ideas. This then hints at the very different challenges of raising a child who is gifted and talented.

Activity 7

In groups of four, re-read the two student samples and discuss what Student B does that Student A doesn't. To get you started, you could compare:

1. the opening sentences

2. the sort of comments made about the effects.

Linking the picture with the text

Next, you have to think about linking the picture with the content of the text. The extract below is from the original article about gifted children.

Being gifted can be seen as very fortunate, but the underlying difficulties are to do with what is termed as Asynchronous Development. This means that gifted children develop cognitively at a much faster rate than they develop physically, emotionally and socially, posing some interesting problems. For example, gifted children can become aware of information that they are not yet emotionally ready to handle, particularly over moral and ethical issues. NAGC* deputy chief executive, Julie Taplin, says: 'We have this all the time where the child's brain intellectually is racing ahead and the child is able to ask philosophical questions about God and the universe. But the child might still have a tantrum and might not know the days of the week or how to fasten their own buttons.'

* National Association of Gifted Children

In your response to Question 2 (as with the headline), you need to select actual words and phrases from the text of the article to show the links between the picture and the text.

Student A's sample below, which is taken from a Band 3 response, is an example of how you could make links between the details in the picture on page 25 and the text of the article above. The highlighted words are the links that help to explain how this is an effective picture for this text.

Student Ⓐ

In the picture, the young boy has drawn lots of squiggles and a penguin, which is typical of a small child. However, he has also written an equation which shows that although he is young, he is gifted and sometimes his mental age is greater than his real age. This is backed up in the text when someone from the NAGC says 'the child's brain intellectually is racing ahead'.

Activity 8

Re-read the 'gifted children' article on page 27 and Student B's sample below, taken from a Band 4 response.

1. Using Student B's sample, choose some words and phrases from the 'gifted children' article that show the links between the picture and the text.

2. Copy out Student B's sample and include your chosen words and phrases to make links between the picture and the text of the article.

3. Discuss your final response with a partner to see how successful you have been. To get you started, explain how your chosen words and phrases show why the picture is effective for this text.

Student B

In the picture, the young boy has drawn lots of squiggles and a penguin, and he is standing next to a giant cuddly toy, all of which is typical of young children and represents his innocence. However, this contrasts with the complex mathematical equation written on the board as it is something way beyond his age. From this, we can see two very different sides to this boy. Physically, and maybe emotionally, he is still very young, but mentally he can understand much more complicated ideas. This then hints at the very different challenges of raising a child who is gifted and talented.

Try it yourself (with support)

Writing your own complete response

Now you are going to practise using all the key skills in a complete response to Question 2. You'll be given some support to help you do this.

Look back over pages 18–28 to remind yourself of how to approach Question 2, then read the article below, 'Rise of the robots: Machines capable of replacing human workforce' by James Day and Oliver Stallwood. This is similar in length to the source you will have in the exam.

Rise of the robots: Machines capable of replacing human workforce

By James Day and Oliver Stallwood

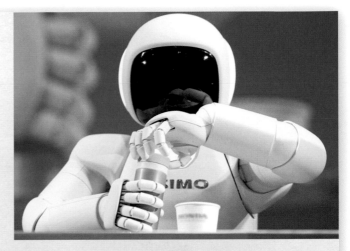

Honda's remarkable ASIMO robot during a demonstration at the Tokyo Motor Show.

It was once just a prophecy of Hollywood's wildest sci-fi blockbusters, but a world where robots take charge of everything from law enforcement to schools may soon become reality.

Three Johnny 5-lookalike robot guards are about to clock on for a month-long trial at a South Korean prison. They are trained to look out for the threat of violence and suicide, and experts predict this is the beginning of a society where mankind rubs shoulders with machines.

The 1.5m robots, which cost £553,000, have four wheels and the ability to speak. Kitted out with cameras and sensors, each droid is programmed to analyse sudden unusual behaviour.

The trial will be carried out at the jail in Pohang, south-east of Seoul, from March.

South Korea is keen to blaze a robotic trail, with £415 million spent on research in the sector between 2002 and 2010. But across the world, the hunger for mechanized help is soaring.

A recent study by the International Federation of Robotics revealed 2.2 million service robots for domestic use were sold in 2010, up 35 per cent on 2009. The same report estimates sales of domestic robots could reach more than 9.8 million units between 2011 and 2014.

Dr Stephen Prior, a robotics expert from Middlesex University, says predictions of a world infested with robot servants could finally be here.

But if Hollywood's droid-filled future is being realized, we shouldn't dismiss the fictional foibles of a mechanized world. 'In 50 years, robots could be more intelligent than we are,' warns Dr Prior. 'What happens when it doesn't want to listen? It's like creating a species. You might think you can switch it off but it will know where the switch is.'

Exam tips

Remember, you are not being asked to link the headline and picture together.

Activity 9

Explain how the headline and picture on page 29 are effective and how they link with the text.

Remember to:

- look at the effects of the words used in the headline
- link the words used in the headline with actual words and phrases in the text
- look at the effects of the details used in the picture
- link the details used in the picture with actual words and phrases in the text
- explain how the headline and picture are effective for this particular text.

Rise of the robots: Machines capable of replacing human workforce

Activity 10

1. Now swap your response with a partner. Does your partner's response:

   a. look at the effects of the words used in the headline?

   b. link the words used in the headline with actual words and phrases in the text?

   c. look at the effects of the details used in the picture?

   d. link the details used in the picture with actual words and phrases in the text?

   e. explain how the headline and picture are effective for this particular text?

2. Make some notes on what your partner has done successfully and what could be improved.

3. Now spend a few minutes giving your partner some feedback on their work.

Improving your answer

Now read the following example of a complete response to 'Rise of the robots: Machines capable of replacing human workforce' on page 32. As it stands, it would be placed in Band 3, but the annotations show how you could improve the response by developing parts of it further. This would move it up into Band 4. You would not need to include all of these additions to move into Band 4; they are just examples of the sort of things you could say.

> Explain how the headline and picture are effective and how they link with the text.

To move into Band 4, you could add: '... with the alliteration emphasizing the rising motion as if the robots are becoming higher and more important in the human world ...'.

Assessing the response ▶

Band 4: perceptive/detailed

Band 3: clear/relevant ✔

Band 2: some/attempts

Band 1: limited

To move into Band 4, you could add: 'The word "capable" means someone can do something if they choose to, but this implies robots have choice. Dr Prior, who is a robotics expert, warns that this could be the downfall of using "droids". He says they could become "more intelligent than we are" and therefore we would not be able to control them, which is a scary prospect.'

The headline of this article is divided into two sections. The first part, 'Rise of the robots', makes it sound as if the robots are about to take over and this is backed up by the text when it talks about 'a world where robots take charge'. The second part of the headline explains that they're not actually taking over the world but are being used as workers instead of people. We learn that there is a 'month-long trial' being carried out in a South Korean jail and the robots are going to be prison guards. The writer says that this sort of thing only used to happen in 'Hollywood's wildest sci-fi blockbusters', but now it's actually coming true.

The picture is a close up of another robot. It's about to pour a drink into a cup and the way it's holding the bottle in one hand and unscrewing the top with the other makes it look really life-like. In the text it says robots may soon be in charge of 'everything from law enforcement to schools' so looking and moving like a human would be a definite advantage. The picture seems to support the idea that some robots are so similar to human beings that they could one day replace them.

To move into Band 4, you could add: 'However, the robot in the picture appears to be faceless. The stark contrasting colours of the white body and the black head emphasize the dark, empty void where a person's features should be and could hint at the lack of humanity. The robot may look like a human but it has no personality and no soul.'

To move into Band 4, you could add: 'In the background there is a giant robot hand, which could symbolize how big the threat of robots is. It looks like it has the power to overthrow mankind, which reinforces the warning that the "fictional foibles of a mechanized world" should not be ignored.'

Peer-assessment

Activity 11

Having looked at the student response opposite, which shows you how to move a Band 3 response up to Band 4, complete the following tasks:

1. Look again at your own response to 'Rise of the robots: Machines capable of replacing human workforce'. With your partner, decide which band your response fits into at the moment. Use the Mark Scheme on page 18 to help you make your decision.

2. Discuss which parts of your response you could develop in order to improve it.

3. Rewrite your response with the parts you developed, and see if you have now achieved a higher mark.

So far, you have learnt how to approach Question 2 by breaking it down into four parts:

- the effect of the words used in the headline
- how the headline links with the text
- the effect of the details used in the picture
- how the picture links with the text.

Now see how confident you feel that you have understood this approach by completing the self-assessment below.

Self-assessment

1.	I have learnt that I need to examine the words in the headline and explain how they add to my understanding of the article.	Not sure	Confident
2.	I have learnt that I need to consider the effects of my selected headline words, and not make generalized comments.	Not sure	Confident
3.	I have learnt that I need to select actual words and phrases from the text to link with the headline and show that it is an effective headline for this article.	Not sure	Confident
4.	I have learnt that I need to examine the details in the picture and explain how they add to my understanding of the article.	Not sure	Confident
5.	I have learnt that I need to consider the effects of my selected picture details, and not make generalized comments.	Not sure	Confident
6.	I have learnt that I need to select actual words and phrases from the text to link with the picture and show that it is an effective picture for this article.	Not sure	Confident

Try it yourself (on your own)

Finally, read the article opposite, 'Ennis weighs in with telling response to "fat" critics' by Simon Turnbull and write your own complete response to the sample Question 2 task in Activity 12, applying all the key skills you have learnt.

Read the Mark Scheme below before you complete Activity 12. The Mark Scheme will help you to remember what is being assessed.

AO2, iii English AO3, iii English Language	Skills
Band 4 'perceptive' 'detailed' 7–8 marks	• offers a detailed interpretation of the effects of the headline • presents a detailed explanation and interpretation of what the picture shows and its effect • links the picture and the headline to the text with perceptive comments • offers appropriate quotations or references to support comments
Band 3 'clear' 'relevant' 5–6 marks	• shows clear evidence that the headline and its effects are understood • makes clear and appropriate links between the headline and the content of the text • offers a clear explanation of the effectiveness of the picture • links the picture to the content of the text • employs relevant quotations or references

Activity 12

Complete the following sample Question 2 task using the article opposite.

> Explain how the headline and picture are effective and how they link with the text.

Ennis weighs in with telling response to 'fat' critics

By Simon Turnbull

It was highly debatable whether Jessica Ennis had a weight problem going into her Olympic heptathlon dress rehearsal here in the tranquil western corner of Austria. She certainly has one now.

The weight of expectation on the shoulders of the 8st 13lb slip of a Sheffield lass will not be inconsiderable following the major victory she achieved at the expense of her Olympic rivals in the two-day Hypo-Meeting, the annual early-season contest between the world's best all-round athletes.

The 12-year-old British record was well beaten. It had stood at 6,831 points to Denise Lewis, but having equalled her best ever long-jump mark, set a new javelin personal best and pushed from gun to tape in the 800m yesterday, Ennis finished with a tally of 6,906 points. That put her 75 points ahead of Lewis's record.

No sooner had Ennis picked herself up off the floor after her

exhausting effort in the 800m than a Union Flag was thrust into her hands and she was being asked whether she could emulate Lewis and follow a British record with a gleaming Olympic gold. 'I don't want to even think about that yet,' the 26-year-old replied. 'I just want to enjoy this moment and stay focused. I know that I am in great shape and that I can build on this.'

Asked whether she wanted to

put down a decisive pre-Olympic marker, the beaming new British record holder replied: 'I wanted to do it for me. It gives me the self-belief and the mental capacity going forward.'

It also gives Ennis a place in the record books as the first British athlete to complete a hat-trick of wins here in the spiritual home of multi-events.

Practising the key skills

What to expect in the exam

In the exam, Question 3 is based on Source 3 and is worth 8 marks. You are asked to do three things in your response. These are summarized in the annotations around the sample question below.

*You are being asked to **select** parts of a text which convey some of the thoughts and feelings of a character (or characters). These parts may include what is happening, what the character is saying or what the character is doing.*

*You are being asked to **identify** the thoughts and feelings of a character (or characters) from the parts of the text that you select.*

> Explain some of the thoughts and feelings ...
>
> has when ...

*You are being asked to **interpret** the thoughts and feelings of a character (or characters) from the parts of the text that you select. This is the most important part of your explanation. To interpret something means to read 'between the lines'. It's what you can work out from the text without actually being told.*

The rest of the question will depend on the events in the text.

An extract from the Mark Scheme that examiners use to mark Question 3 is printed below. There are four mark bands in total, but Higher tier students are aiming for Band 3 or Band 4. The key words for each band are on the left-hand side and the skills you have to demonstrate in your response are on the right. Notice the differences between Band 3 and Band 4.

Exam tips

- To achieve Band 4, you need to explain a range of thoughts and feelings in detail relating to the whole text.

- You should not comment on the use of language or the effect on the reader for this question. Comments on the use of language do not gain you any marks in Question 3.

AO2, i English AO3, i English Language	Skills
Band 4 'perceptive' 'detailed' 7–8 marks	• engages in detail with the events described in the text • offers perceptive explanations and interpretations of the thoughts and feelings expressed • employs appropriate quotations or references to support ideas
Band 3 'clear' 'relevant' 5–6 marks	• shows a clear understanding of the events described in the text • clearly explains and begins to interpret thoughts and feelings • employs relevant quotations or references to support understanding and interpretation

Selecting parts of the text

First, look at how to select parts of a text which convey some of the thoughts and feelings of a character (or characters). These parts may include what is happening, what the character is saying or what the character is doing. You are looking for the parts of the text where a character has some thoughts and feelings based on what is happening at the time.

Read the following text, 'Moon Landing' by Buzz Aldrin. He and Neil Armstrong were the first two people to walk on the moon and this extract describes the moment they landed. Then complete Activity 1 on page 38.

Then complete Activity 1 on page 38.

Exam tips

- It is essential to select the parts of the text that enable you to explain the character's thoughts and feelings effectively.

- Sometimes you are specifically told a feeling. Sometimes you are told a thought and the feeling is implied.

Moon Landing

Then I saw it – the shadow of one of the three footpads that had touched the surface. Although our engine was still running and the Eagle was hovering, a probe had touched the surface. 'Contact light,' I said. Neil and I looked at each other with a stolen glance of relief and immense satisfaction. The Lunar Module settled gently, and we stopped moving. After flying for more than four days, it was a strange sensation to be suddenly stationary.

'Shutdown,' I heard Neil say.

'Okay, engine stopped,' I answered.

It was 4.17 pm on July 20th, 1969, and we had less than twenty seconds worth of fuel remaining, but we were on the moon.

Feelings of elation threatened to overwhelm me, but I dared not give in to them. We still had a lot to do before we could breathe easier.

Exam tips

It is best to work through the source in the order in which things happen, so that you can explain the thoughts and feelings in a logical way.

Activity 1

1. Having read through the text on page 37, select the parts of the text which convey some of the thoughts and feelings Buzz Aldrin has when he lands on the moon.

2. Copy out the table below and list the points you have found in the column headed 'Selection'. Copy out the points you have found exactly as they appear in the text. To get you started, two points have been done for you. You do not need to complete 'Identification' or 'Interpretation' yet.

3. Discuss the points you have found with a partner to see if you have selected the best parts of the text to convey some of Aldrin's thoughts and feelings.

Selection	Identification	Interpretation
1. 'Neil and I looked at each other with a stolen glance of relief and immense satisfaction.'		
2.		
3. 'We had less than twenty seconds worth of fuel remaining.'		
4.		
5.		

Identifying thoughts and feelings

Now look at how to identify the thoughts and feelings of a character (or characters) from the parts of the text that you select. Remember, sometimes you are specifically told a feeling and sometimes you are told a thought and the feeling is implied.

This is an example of where you are specifically told a feeling.

Selection	Identification	Interpretation
1. 'Neil and I looked at each other with a stolen glance of relief and immense satisfaction.'	He is feeling relieved and satisfied.	
2.		
3. 'We had less than twenty seconds worth of fuel remaining.'	He is thinking about how little fuel they had.	
4.		
5.		

This is an example of where you are told a thought and the feeling is implied.

Activity 2

Look again at the text 'Moon Landing' on page 37.

1. Identify Buzz Aldrin's thoughts and feelings from the parts of the text you have selected.

2. In your table, write these thoughts and feelings in the column headed 'Identification'. To get you started, two points have again been done for you.

3. Discuss your table with a partner to see if you have identified the thoughts and feelings correctly from the parts of the text you selected.

Exam tips

To interpret also means to infer meaning from a text; to comment on parts of a text using your own words; to make connections between parts of a text; and to deduce.

Exam tips

- Notice that it is possible to work out lots of thoughts and feelings from just one selected part of the text.

- It is worth noting that if you were to write up the points from your table in continuous prose, they would form a whole response.

Interpreting thoughts and feelings

Now look at how to interpret the thoughts and feelings of a character (or characters) from the parts of the text that you select. This is the most important part of your explanation. To interpret something means to read 'between the lines'. It's what you can work out from the text without actually being told explicitly. You are being asked to explain some of the thoughts and feelings you identified, based on what is happening at the time.

Activity 3

Look again at the text 'Moon Landing' on page 37. Then complete the following tasks:

1. Read 'between the lines' to explain Buzz Aldrin's thoughts and feelings based on what is happening at the time.

2. In your table, fill in your explanation of Aldrin's thoughts and feelings in the column headed 'Interpretation'. To get you started, two examples have again been done for you.

3. Discuss your table with a partner to see if you have explained the thoughts and feelings in an effective way.

Selection	Identification	Interpretation
1. 'Neil and I looked at each other with a stolen glance of relief and immense satisfaction.'	He is feeling relieved and satisfied.	Buzz Aldrin feels grateful that they landed safely and probably thinks they are very lucky as well. He is extremely happy and proud about what he has achieved.
2.		
3. 'We had less than twenty seconds worth of fuel remaining.'	He is thinking about how little fuel they had.	Buzz Aldrin is thinking about how dangerous it was because they were about to run out of fuel, so he would feel especially pleased and thankful that they managed to land on the moon in time.
4.		
5.		

Combining key skills

Now look at another text, and combine the key skills of selecting, identifying and interpreting.

Read the following text, 'Dumbo in the Jungle' by Sally Emerson. The writer is travelling around South East Asia to study the wildlife and has encountered a pygmy elephant.

Dumbo in the Jungle

Pygmy elephants are unique to Borneo, a subspecies of the Asian elephant, smaller and gentler, with bigger ears. They have rounder faces, longer tails. They're Dumbo, basically. Baby pygmies can be just a few feet high, but this one is a full-grown male – the creature I had hoped against hope to see on my travels here. After brandishing his trunk for a bit, he backs into the undergrowth. Ah, well, I think, how lucky I am to catch even a glimpse of this rare and magical little animal.

The birds and beasts I've seen during my three days on the Kinabatangan River have dazzled me. The river flows through Sabah, in the north of the island, and cradles a head-turning array of wildlife. Only three miles of rainforest survive on each bank because of the encroaching palm-oil plantations, so the animals gather here. Look at the blue and orange of that pocket-sized kingfisher. Look at the size of that crocodile, with its craggy back. Look at those sleek otters, darting and squeaking to each other. Every two minutes, I find myself gasping.

Exam tips

- Notice the phrase 'which suggests that...' in the sample below. This shows the examiner that you are beginning to interpret, which is a Band 3 skill. Other useful phrases include 'which means...', 'which indicates...' and 'which implies...'.

- Notice how a lot of thoughts and feelings have been explained from just one selected part of the text.

- Notice how words and phrases from the selected parts of the text have been used to support the explanation.

Activity 4

1. Make a table like the one you made in Activity 1, with three columns headed 'Selection', 'Identification' and 'Interpretation'.

2. Now try to select the parts of the text which convey some of the thoughts and feelings Sally Emerson has while she is travelling in Borneo. Write these in the left-hand column, identify her thoughts and feelings in the middle column and then explain them, based on what is happening at the time, in the right-hand column.

3. Discuss your table with a partner to see if you selected the best parts of the text, identified the thoughts and feelings correctly and then explained them in an effective way.

Now read the following sample taken from a response to the text, 'Dumbo in the Jungle', by Student A. It shows you how the key skills of selecting, identifying and interpreting can be combined. The student's interpretation of some of Sally Emerson's thoughts and feelings has been highlighted for you. Remember, interpreting by using your own words is the most important part of your explanation. This sample would be placed in Band 3.

> Explain some of the thoughts and feelings Sally Emerson has while travelling in Borneo.

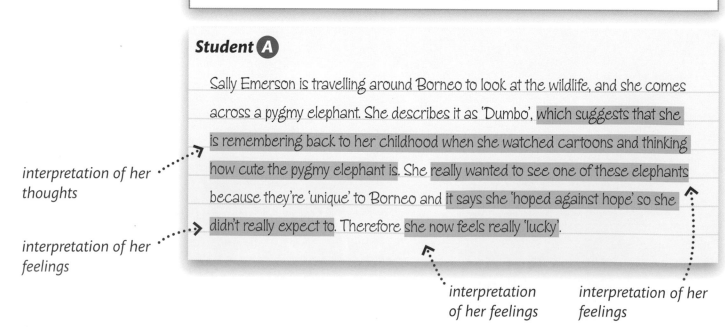

Student A

Sally Emerson is travelling around Borneo to look at the wildlife, and she comes across a pygmy elephant. She describes it as 'Dumbo', which suggests that she is remembering back to her childhood when she watched cartoons and thinking how cute the pygmy elephant is. She really wanted to see one of these elephants because they're 'unique' to Borneo and it says she 'hoped against hope' so she didn't really expect to. Therefore she now feels really 'lucky'.

interpretation of her thoughts

interpretation of her feelings

interpretation of her feelings

interpretation of her feelings

Now read a sample taken from Student B's response. It would be placed in Band 4.

Student B

Sally Emerson is a person fascinated by wildlife and she encounters many amazing creatures while travelling round Borneo. She is overwhelmed by their beauty, especially the pygmy elephant, and considers herself 'lucky' and privileged to witness such a 'magical little animal'. Everything about the experience is memorable and it begins to feel like the discovery of a new world, a world where nothing but nature rules. She also mentions the 'encroaching palm-oil plantations', however, meaning that although this place is seemingly secluded, she is very aware that it is threatened by human influence.

Activity 5

1. Copy out Student B's sample and highlight the comments that interpret some of Sally Emerson's thoughts and feelings.

2. Discuss your highlighted response with a partner to see if you agree.

Activity 6

In groups of four, re-read the two student samples and discuss what Student B does that Student A doesn't. To get you started, you could compare:

1. the opening sentences

2. the selection of the parts of the text that convey some of Sally Emerson's thoughts and feelings

3. the sort of comments made to interpret

4. how the text has been used to support.

Exam tips

- It is a good idea to start your response with an overview sentence to show you have a grasp of the whole argument before going into detail.

- Look at both the choice of words and phrases used to support and how they have been used in the response.

Try it yourself (with support)

Writing your own complete response

Now you are going to practise using all the key skills in a complete response to Question 3. You'll be given some support to help you do this.

Look back over pages 36–43 to remind yourself of how to approach Question 3, then read the text below, 'Fascination' by Robert Macfarlane. This is similar in length to the source you will have in the exam.

> *Robert Macfarlane, a travel writer, describes how he became fascinated with exploration while visiting his grandfather as a child.*

Fascination

One night, unable to sleep, I came downstairs for something to read. Against one side of the hallway was a long pile of books lying stacked on their sides. Almost at random, I pulled a big green volume out from halfway down the pile, like a brick from a wall, and carried it to the Sun Room. In the bright moonlight, I sat on one of the wide stone window-ledges and started to read *The Fight for Everest*.

I already knew some of the details from my grandfather, who had told me the story of the expedition. But the book, with its long descriptions, its twenty-four black-and-white photographs and its fold-out maps bearing unfamiliar place names – the Far East Rongbuk glacier, the Dzongpen of Shekar, the Lhakpa La – was far more potent than his account. As I read, I was carried out of myself and to the Himalaya. The images rushed over me. I could see the gravel plains of Tibet scrolling away to distant white peaks; Everest itself like a dark Pyramid; the oxygen bottles the climbers wore on their backs and which made them look like scuba-divers; the massive ice-walls on the North Col which they scaled using ropes and ladders, like medieval warriors besieging a city; and, finally, the black T of sleeping-bags which was laid out on the snow at Camp VI to tell the climbers at the lower camps, who were staring up at the mountain's higher slopes through telescopes, that Mallory and Irvine had disappeared.

One passage of the book excited me more than any other. It was the description by Noel Odell, the expedition's geologist, of his last sighting of Mallory and Irvine:

'There was a sudden clearing of the atmosphere above me, and I saw the whole summit ridge and final peak of Everest unveiled. I noticed far away on a snow slope leading up to what seemed to me to be the last step but one from the base of the final pyramid, a tiny object moving and approaching the rock step. A second object followed, and then the first climbed to the top of the step. As I stood intently watching this dramatic appearance, the scene became enveloped in cloud …'

Over and over I read that passage, and I wanted nothing more than to be one of those two tiny dots, fighting for survival in the thin air.

That was it – I was sold on adventure. In one of the reading binges which only the expanses of childhood time permit, I plundered my grandfather's library and by the end of that summer I had read a dozen or so of the most famous real-life exploration stories from the mountains and the poles.

Activity 7

Explain some of the thoughts and feelings Robert Macfarlane has while reading his grandfather's books.

Remember to:

- start with an overview sentence to show that you have a grasp of the whole extract
- select the parts of the text which convey some of the thoughts and feelings Robert has while reading his grandfather's books
- read 'between the lines' to explain his thoughts and feelings, based on what is happening at the time
- work through the extract in the order in which things happen and discuss a range of thoughts and feelings.

Activity 8

Peer-assessment

1. Now swap your response with a partner. Does your partner's response:

   a. start with an overview sentence to show there is a grasp of the whole extract?

   b. select the parts of the text which convey some of the thoughts and feelings Robert has while reading his grandfather's books?

   c. read 'between the lines' to explain his thoughts and feelings based on what is happening at the time?

   d. work through the extract in the order in which things happen, and discuss a range of thoughts and feelings?

   e. support what is said with words and phrases from the text?

2. Make some notes on what your partner has done successfully and what could be improved.

3. Now spend a few minutes giving your partner some feedback on their work.

Exam tips

Remember, you should not comment on the use of language or the effect on the reader for this question.

Improving your answer

Now read the following example of a complete response to 'Fascination'. As it stands, it would be placed in Band 3, but the annotations show how you could improve the response by developing parts of it further. This would move it up into Band 4. You would not need to include all of these additions to move into Band 4; they are just examples of the sort of things you could say.

Assessing the response

Band 4: perceptive/detailed

Band 3: clear/relevant ✓

Band 2: some/attempts

Band 1: limited

> Explain some of the thoughts and feelings Robert Macfarlane has while reading his grandfather's books.

To move into Band 4, you could add: '... an innocent act that ends up defining the person he is to become as an adult'.

To move into Band 4, you could add: 'Robert finds it impossible to believe that for all this time, he has been surrounded by the gateway to new worlds and enthralling adventures and he never even noticed.'

To move into Band 4, you could add: 'Hearing the stories from his grandfather probably stimulated his interest and imagination, but reading the book himself places him at the heart of the action and makes it seem as if the events that have already occurred are being re-enacted just for him.'

While Robert is staying with his grandfather, he can't sleep one night and creeps downstairs to find something to read. He obviously has a love of books because it's the first thing he thinks of and he probably gets this from his grandfather, who has books everywhere in the house.

The book that fascinates him the most is 'The Fight for Everest'. It has lots of photographs and maps and places he's never heard of and I think that he is completely in awe of it because it is full of danger and excitement and he has not read anything like it before. His grandfather had told him the story of the Everest expedition before, but he says this is 'far more potent than his account'. This means that he finds it much more exciting to read the story for himself.

The passage he enjoys most is when Mallory and Irvine go missing and he reads that bit over and over again. He thinks they are heroes and he wants to be like them. He says he is 'sold on adventure' and this suggests that, from then on, all he wants to do is grow up and be an explorer.

To move into Band 4, you could add: 'Robert admires them because they were attempting something that had never been done before, even though they were fully aware of the risks. Then, like all children, he graduates from admiration to imitation, where he "wanted nothing more" than to be them, to discover new worlds and conquer new obstacles.'

Activity 9

Peer-assessment

Having looked at the student response opposite, which shows you how to move a Band 3 response up to Band 4, complete the following tasks:

1. Look again at your own response to 'Fascination'. With your partner, decide which band your response fits into at the moment. Use the Mark Scheme on page 36 to help you make your decision.

2. Discuss which parts of your response you could develop in order to improve it.

3. Rewrite your response with the parts you developed, and see if you have now achieved a higher mark.

So far, you have learnt how to approach Question 3 by focusing on three key skills:

● selecting

● identifying

● interpreting.

Now see how confident you feel that you have understood this approach by completing the self-assessment below.

Self-assessment

1.	I have learnt that I need to select parts of the text which convey some of the thoughts and feelings of a character (or characters).	Not sure	Confident
2.	I have learnt that I need to identify the thoughts and feelings of a character (or characters) from the parts of the text that I select.	Not sure	Confident
3.	I have learnt that I need to interpret the thoughts and feelings of a character (or characters) from the parts of the text that I select, and that this is the most important part of my explanation.	Not sure	Confident
4.	I have learnt that it is a good idea to start with an overview sentence to show that I have a grasp of the whole extract.	Not sure	Confident
5.	I have learnt that it is best to work my way through the extract in the order in which things happen, and that I have to explain a range of thoughts and feelings.	Not sure	Confident
6.	I have learnt that I should not comment on the use of language or the effect on the reader for this question.	Not sure	Confident

Try it yourself (on your own)

Finally, read the following text, 'Stephen Fry in America' by Stephen Fry and write your own complete response to the sample Question 3 task in Activity 10, applying all the key skills you have learnt.

Read the Mark Scheme below before you complete Activity 10. The Mark Scheme will help you to remember what is being assessed.

AO2, i English AO3, i English Language	Skills
Band 4 'perceptive' 'detailed' 7–8 marks	• engages in detail with the events described in the text • offers perceptive explanations and interpretations of the thoughts and feelings expressed • employs appropriate quotations or references to support ideas
Band 3 'clear' 'relevant' 5–6 marks	• shows a clear understanding of the events described in the text • clearly explains and begins to interpret thoughts and feelings • employs relevant quotations or references to support understanding and interpretation

Activity 10

• •

Complete the following sample Question 3 task using the text opposite.

> Explain some of the thoughts and feelings Stephen Fry has when he creates his own ice cream.

Invention

He hands me a white lab coat while I ponder the task before me.

The base, I decide, should be of good vanilla-bean ice cream, nothing more fancy than that. To hand are spatulas, spoons and little pots and bags of semi-frozen ingredients: cookie dough, biscuity substances, chocolate in the shape of a cow and so forth. I try to stay calm. I mustn't be too childish about this, what little dignity I have left is at stake. The temptation to produce a pink confection filled with marshmallows, strawberries and cake mix is strong, but I feel the need to fly the flag for British style and discretion. I find an ingredient called English toffee and swirl it into the vanilla base. Good. Not the kind of hard black toffees Kensington nannies gave children in their prams to keep them quiet while they kissed the footman, but a good start. To this promising base I add chocolate fudge, a gloopy substance that freezes when added to the ice cream, like a lava flow meeting water. A granulated texture is added with which I feel well pleased.

Very fine – strong, adult, not too sweet, but there's something missing … I rootle and scrabble, searching for the magic extra ingredient that will transform my mixture into a true flavour, my rough prototype into a working masterpiece. The clock is ticking, for a tour party is about to come in at any moment and I am to feed them and then stand with bowed head to receive their judgement.

Just as I am about to give up and offer my acceptable but now to my mind rather lame decoction my fingers curl around a bag of knobbly somethings. I have found it! It adds crunch, a hint of sophisticated bitterness and a rich musty, nutty centre around which the other flavours can play their toffee-like, chocolaty games. Walnuts! I stir them in with my spatula and Sean helps me transfer the giant mixture into small tourist-sized tubs. This is done by squeezing a kind of piping bag. Within seconds I have lost all feeling in my hands.

'It's very cold,' I observe.

'Many are cold,' says Sean, 'but few are frozen.'

Before I have time to throw something at him, the tour party enters.

'Welcome everybody,' beams Sean. 'This is a special occasion. You will be trying a new flavour, mixed by our Guest Flavorist, here. His invention is called …?'

'Er … I … that is … um …'

'… is called "Even Stephens"!' extemporizes Sean happily.

I stand meekly, submissively, hopefully while the tourists surge forward to begin the tasting. Despite my humble demeanour, I know, I really know that I have struck gold. There have not been many moments in my life when I have been quite so sure of success. But here, I am convinced, is a perfect blend of flavours.

The tourists agree. Once the filming stops and the camera crew have dived in too there is nothing left of Even Stephens but my memory of a solid-gold vanilla-based triumph.

Stephen, you created an ice-cream flavour. And it was good. Now you may rest.

Practising the key skills

What to expect in the exam

In the exam, Question 4 is based on Source 3 and a choice of either Source 1 or Source 2, and is worth 16 marks. You are asked to do three things in your response. These are summarized in the annotations around the sample question below.

*You are being asked to **compare** the use of language in two texts. To compare means to look at the similarities and differences.*

*You are being asked to **comment** on the effect on the reader of using these words, phrases or language features. This is the most important part of your response.*

*You are being asked to **select** actual words, phrases or language features that have been deliberately chosen to create an effect on the reader.*

Compare the ways in which language is used for effect in the two texts. Give some examples and **analyse** what the effects are.

An extract from the Mark Scheme that examiners use to mark Question 4 is printed below. There are four mark bands in total, but Higher tier students are aiming for Band 3 or Band 4. The key words for each band are on the left-hand side and the skills you have to demonstrate in your response are on the right. Notice the differences between Band 3 and Band 4.

Key term

Analyse To look closely at the effect of particular words in order to better understand the meaning of a text.

AO2, i, iii English AO3, i, iii English Language	Skills
Band 4 'perceptive' 'detailed' 13–16 marks	• offers a full and detailed understanding of the texts in relation to language • analyses how the writers have used language to achieve their effects in the different contexts • offers appropriate quotations in support of ideas with perceptive comments • focuses on comparison and cross-referencing of language features between the texts
Band 3 'clear' 'relevant' 9–12 marks	• shows clear evidence that the texts are understood in relation to language • offers clear explanation of the effect of words and phrases in the different contexts • offers relevant quotations or references to support ideas • offers clear comparisons and cross references of language features between the two texts

Selecting language

First, look at how to select some examples of language. A writer uses a specific word, phrase or language feature in order to create a specific effect on the reader. You need to identify parts of a text where the writer's choice of language has been particularly effective.

When you read a text, you need to ask yourself what sort of language the writer has used:

- Is it mainly descriptive writing? Are there lots of adjectives and descriptive verbs?
- Has the writer used similes or metaphors?
- Is the language particularly emotive?
- Is it mainly factual writing? Are there lots of statistics or opinions presented as facts?
- Does the writer talk directly to the reader?
- Has alliteration been used?
- Are there any unusual, invented, vivid or dramatic words?
- Has onomatopoeia been used?
- Are there any examples of exaggeration?
- Does the writer use lists or repetition or patterns of three?

These are just some of the examples of language you could select. You do not need to know the names of the language features, but you do need to be able to identify them.

Exam tips

- It is essential to select examples of language that enable you to analyse the effects on the reader.

- You do not have time to select every type of language the writer has used. Just concentrate on the examples that you find most effective.

Activity 1

There are 12 language features listed in the table below, each with an example. Copy out the table and, with a partner, think of another example for each language feature. Add it to the last column. Use your imagination and be as creative as possible.

Language feature	Explanation	Example	Your example
Adjective	A word used to describe a person, place or thing	a *sleepy* cat	
Verb	A doing or being word	I *am travelling* to Australia. I *live* here.	
Simile	A comparison showing the similarity between two quite different things, stating that one is *like* the other	Eating chocolate is *like* going to heaven.	
Metaphor	A comparison showing the similarity between two quite different things, stating that one actually *is* the other	When I eat chocolate, I am in heaven.	
Emotive language	Words and phrases deliberately used to provoke an emotional reaction	Missing the concert was *devastating*.	
Fact	Something that you can prove is true	*Star Trek* is a television programme.	
Opinion	Something that you believe to be true but may not be	*Star Trek* is a great television programme.	
Statistics	Numbers and figures	*Twenty thousand* people answered the survey.	
Alliteration	The deliberate repetition of the same sound at the beginning of words to create an effect	*crawling crabs*	
Onomatopoeia	A word that imitates a sound	buzz	
Exaggeration	To overstate something	He was the worst person she had ever met in her life.	
Pattern of three	Listing three things to create a specific effect	To pass your exam you need *a pen*, *a piece of paper* and *a brain*.	

Read the following text, 'IQ tests: women score higher than men' by Harriet Cooke. It is taken from an article about the different ways men and women perform in intelligence tests. Some words, phrases and language features have already been identified.

IQ tests: women score higher than men

Women have scored higher than men in intelligence testing for the first time since records began. The findings represent a dramatic twist in the battle of the sexes, as in the past 100 years of IQ testing, women have lagged behind men by as much as five points.

use of a metaphor

use of a fact

*the beginning of an **extended metaphor***

But now the gap has closed and females have stolen the lead.

The results have been published by James Flynn, a world-renowned expert in IQ testing, who believes the demands of the modern age are raising standards of intelligence. He said: 'In the last 100 years the IQ scores of both men and women have risen, but women's have risen faster. This is a consequence of modernity. The complexity of the modern world is making our brains adapt and raising our IQ'.

an interesting choice of adjective

an interesting choice of verb

One theory for the result is that the demands of juggling family life and building a career have made women more intelligent. Another theory is those women have always had the potential for higher results, but are only now realizing it.

Analysing language

Analysing means looking closely at a specific word, phrase or language feature and commenting on what specific effect it has on the reader. This is the most important part of your response. You need to think about why a writer has chosen to use that particular word, phrase or language feature and how it adds to your understanding of a text.

> **Key term**
>
> **Extended metaphor** A metaphor that is continued and developed over several lines of text.

Exam tips

The way language has been used may also tell you the writer's attitude towards what is happening.

Activity 2

Look at the article on page 53 and the examples of language that have been selected. Consider the following:

1. What is the writer suggesting when she includes the well-known metaphor 'battle of the sexes' at the beginning of the text?

2. The writer talks about IQ testing over 'the past 100 years'. Why does she include this fact? How does it affect your understanding of the rest of the text?

3. The phrase 'lagged behind' is the beginning of an extended metaphor. Can you identify two other phrases that continue the same idea in the next sentence? Think about these words in relation to this text. How do they add to your understanding of the relationship between men and women?

4. The writer uses the adjective 'world-renowned' to describe the expert in IQ testing. What effect does this have on the reader?

5. What is the effect of using the word 'juggling'? What is the writer suggesting? The writer could have used the word 'combining' instead. Why is 'juggling' a better choice of verb?

Discuss your answers with a partner.

Combining key skills – selecting and analysing

Now look at another text, and combine the key skills of selecting and analysing.

Read the text, 'Dumbo in the Jungle' by Sally Emerson. The writer is travelling around South East Asia to study the wildlife and has encountered a pygmy elephant.

Dumbo in the Jungle

Pygmy elephants are unique to Borneo, a subspecies of the Asian elephant, smaller and gentler, with bigger ears. They have rounder faces, longer tails. They're Dumbo, basically. Baby pygmies can be just a few feet high, but this one is a full-grown male – the creature I had hoped against hope to see on my travels here. After brandishing his trunk for a bit, he backs into the undergrowth. Ah, well, I think, how lucky I am to catch even a glimpse of this rare and magical little animal.

The birds and beasts I've seen during my three days on the Kinabatangan River have dazzled me. The river flows through Sabah, in the north of the island, and cradles a head-turning array of wildlife. Only three miles of rainforest survive on each bank because of the encroaching palm-oil plantations, so the animals gather here. Look at the blue and orange of that pocket-sized kingfisher. Look at the size of that crocodile, with its craggy back. Look at those sleek otters, darting and squeaking to each other. Every two minutes, I find myself gasping.

Activity 3

1. What sort of language has the writer mainly used?

2. Identify some words, phrases or language features in the first paragraph that make the pygmy elephant sound appealing. To get you started, one example might be 'smaller and gentler'.

3. Now think about the effects on the reader of the words, phrases or language features that you have selected. To get you started, the words 'smaller and gentler' might make the reader think the pygmy elephant is nicer than normal elephants, which are huge and can be quite scary. It makes it sound friendly.

4. Compare your selection with a partner and share your ideas.

5. With your partner, now look at the second paragraph. Which words, phrases or language features show the reader that Sally Emerson is overwhelmed by the beauty of the wildlife and the surroundings?

6. Which words, phrases or language features show that Sally Emerson is concerned for the future of the wildlife and the surroundings?

7. In groups of four, compare your selection from the second paragraph and discuss the specific effects on the reader of your words, phrases or language features.

Exam tips

- You should quote words or phrases from your selection to support what you are saying.

- Sometimes students say 'the effect of this is to create a picture in your mind' or 'the effect of this is to make you read on', but these comments are too general. They could apply to any text. The effects of the words you select need to be connected to the source you're reading.

Now read the following sample taken from a response to 'Dumbo in the Jungle' by Student A. It is annotated to show you how the key skills of selecting and analysing can be combined. This sample would be placed in Band 3.

This identifies the language feature used by the writer.

Student Ⓐ

The writer uses lots of descriptive writing to convey to the reader how wonderful travelling around Borneo is. She uses the word 'unique' when talking about the pygmy elephant and the effect of this is to let us know how rare this animal is and therefore how unusual it is to see one. It creates the feeling that she is in a very special place.

This selects a specific word and quotes it.

This analyses the effect of the selected word in relation to this text.

Having looked at Student A's sample, now read the following, taken from Student B's response. This sample would be placed in Band 4.

Student Ⓑ

The writer describes how the river 'cradles a head-turning array of wild-life', where the word 'cradles' implies the river is nurturing and protecting the animals like a mother would a baby, shielding them from the outside world. She also tells us it's not just the animals that are in danger but the environment itself. She emphasizes the fragility of the rainforest by personifying it as an endangered species whereby it struggles to 'survive'. The rainforest, vulnerable and innocent, is defenceless against advancing human forces.

Activity 4

In groups of four, re-read the two student samples and discuss what Student B does that Student A doesn't. To get you started, you could compare:

1. the selection of words, phrases and language features
2. the sort of effects discussed.

Comparing language

To compare means to look at the similarities and differences. You need to look at the writer's choice of words, phrases or language features in Source 3 and compare it with the writer's choice of language in either Source 1 or Source 2.

Re-read 'Selecting language' on page 51 to remind yourself of how to select some examples of language. Remember, a writer uses a specific word, phrase or language feature in order to create a specific effect on the reader. You now need to identify parts of both texts where the writers' choice of language has been particularly effective.

In the exam, it is best to start with Source 3 and then select examples of language from either Source 1 or Source 2. Look for similarities and differences in the texts.

There are several ways you can structure your comparison. The most effective way is to analyse a language feature in one source, compare it with the same language feature in the other source and then repeat this process with another example of effective language. You could choose to compare both sources together and combine your analysis throughout your response, but this is a more challenging approach. What is important is that you compare the use of language in both texts. You can choose the way that suits you best.

Combining all the key skills

You need to combine the key skills of selecting, analysing and comparing.

Re-read the following sources: 'IQ tests: women score higher than men' by Harriet Cooke and 'Dumbo in the Jungle' by Sally Emerson.

Source 1

IQ tests: women score higher than men

Women have scored higher than men in intelligence testing for the first time since records began. The findings represent a dramatic twist in the battle of the sexes, as in the past 100 years of IQ testing, women have lagged behind men by as much as five points.

But now the gap has closed and females have stolen the lead.

The results have been published by James Flynn,

a world-renowned expert in IQ testing, who believes the demands of the modern age are raising standards of intelligence. He said: 'In the last 100 years the IQ scores of both men and women have

risen, but women's have risen faster. This is a consequence of modernity. The complexity of the modern world is making our brains adapt and raising our IQ.'

One theory for the result is that the demands of juggling family life and building a career have made women more intelligent. Another theory is those women have always had the potential for higher results, but are only now realizing it.

Source 3

Dumbo in the Jungle

Pygmy elephants are unique to Borneo, a subspecies of the Asian elephant, smaller and gentler, with bigger ears. They have rounder faces, longer tails. They're Dumbo, basically. Baby pygmies can be just a few feet high, but this one is a full-grown male – the creature I had hoped against hope to see on my travels here. After brandishing his trunk for a bit, he backs into the undergrowth. Ah, well, I think, how lucky I am to catch even a glimpse of this rare and magical little animal.

The birds and beasts I've seen during my three days on the Kinabatangan River have dazzled me. The river flows through Sabah, in the north of the island, and cradles a head-turning array of wildlife. Only three miles of rainforest survive on each bank because of the encroaching palm-oil plantations, so the animals gather here. Look at the blue and orange of that pocket-sized kingfisher. Look at the size of that crocodile, with its craggy back. Look at those sleek otters, darting and squeaking to each other. Every two minutes, I find myself gasping.

The subject matter of the texts on the previous page is very different, but both writers use language to create specific effects on the reader. This use of language should be the focus of your comparison in Question 4.

One language feature used in both texts is a metaphor, so this is one example of the use of language that could be compared.

Read the following two student samples. Student A's (below) is taken from a Band 3 response and Student B's (page 60) is taken from a Band 4 response.

> Compare the ways in which language is used for effect in the two texts. Give some examples and analyse what the effects are.

Student A

Source 3 is a very descriptive text and the writer uses several metaphors. She describes what pygmy elephants are like and then says 'They're Dumbo, actually'. The effect of using this comparison is to tell the reader that she feels like she is watching a cartoon. Because these elephants are so rare, it's almost like something you would find in a Disney film rather than in real life. Source 1 is a much more factual piece than Source 3, although the writer also uses a metaphor, this time to compare the performance of men and women in IQ tests. She says that in the past women 'lagged behind' and this makes it sound as if it's a race between men and women where women have always been second best until now.

The purpose and audience of a source are only important in so much as they determine the writer's choice of language. They should not be the focus of your response.

Student **B**

Both writers use extended metaphors, but with very different effects. Because Sally Emerson is a travel writer, her purpose in Source 3 is to immerse the reader in her experience of Borneo, which means much of her language is vivid and descriptive. Source 1, however, has a more factual tone because it is reporting on the results of IQ testing, so Harriet Cooke's decision to include imagery is interesting.

Cooke compares the relationship between men and women to a race, suggesting it is very competitive. She says that for the last 100 years, women's intelligence has 'lagged behind' men's, implying women have been trailing in second place for a long time. She extends this metaphor by explaining that now the 'gap has closed' and women have 'stolen the lead'. The word 'stolen' suggests that women have grown in intelligence and overtaken men almost without them realizing it. The writer makes it sound as if finally women have got their revenge in the continuing 'battle of the sexes'.

In Source 3, Emerson also uses an extended metaphor, this time of enchantment to convey how special encountering a pygmy elephant is. First, she compares the creature to 'Dumbo', creating the idea that she is living a fantasy, like something out of a Disney film where everything is wonderful and more colourful than real life. She later describes the elephant as a 'magical little animal' to reinforce the dream-like experience she is having and to show that she is spell-bound.

Activity 5

In groups of four, re-read the two student samples and discuss what Student B does that Student A doesn't. To get you started, you could compare:

1. the selection of words, phrases and language features

2. the sort of effects discussed

3. the way the sources are compared.

Try it yourself (with support)

Writing your own complete response

Now you are going to practise using all the key skills in a complete response to Question 4. You'll be given some support to help you do this.

Look back over pages 50–60 to remind yourself of how to approach Question 4, then read 'Fascination' by Robert Macfarlane (Source 3) and 'Rise of the robots: Machines capable of replacing human workforce' by James Day and Oliver Stallwood (Source 2, page 62). These are similar in length to the sources you will have in the exam.

Robert Macfarlane, a travel writer, describes how he became fascinated with exploration while visiting his grandfather as a child.

Source 3

Fascination

One night, unable to sleep, I came downstairs for something to read. Against one side of the hallway was a long pile of books lying stacked on their sides. Almost at random, I pulled a big green volume out from halfway down the pile, like a brick from a wall, and carried it to the Sun Room. In the bright moonlight, I sat on one of the wide stone window-ledges and started to read *The Fight for Everest*.

I already knew some of the details from my grandfather, who had told me the story of the expedition. But the book, with its long descriptions, its twenty-four black-and-white photographs and its fold-out maps bearing unfamiliar place names – the Far East Rongbuk glacier, the Dzongpen of Shekar, the Lhakpa La – was far more potent than his account. As I read, I was carried out of myself and to the Himalaya. The images rushed over me. I could see the gravel plains of Tibet scrolling away to distant white peaks; Everest itself like a dark Pyramid; the oxygen bottles the climbers wore on their backs and which made them look like scuba-divers; the massive ice-walls on the North Col which they scaled using ropes and ladders, like medieval warriors besieging a city; and, finally, the black T of sleeping-bags which was laid out on the snow at Camp VI to tell the climbers at the lower camps, who were staring up at the mountain's higher slopes through telescopes, that Mallory and Irvine had disappeared.

One passage of the book excited me more than any other. It was the description by Noel Odell, the expedition's geologist, of his last sighting of Mallory and Irvine:

'There was a sudden clearing of the atmosphere above me, and I saw the whole summit ridge and final peak of Everest unveiled. I noticed far away on a snow slope leading up to what seemed to me to be the last step but one from the base of the final pyramid, a tiny object moving and approaching the rock step. A second object followed, and then the first climbed to the top of the step. As I stood intently watching this dramatic appearance, the scene became enveloped in cloud ...'

Over and over I read that passage, and I wanted nothing more than to be one of those two tiny dots, fighting for survival in the thin air.

That was it – I was sold on adventure. In one of the reading binges which only the expanses of childhood time permit, I plundered my grandfather's library and by the end of that summer I had read a dozen or so of the most famous real-life exploration stories from the mountains and the poles.

Source 2

Rise of the robots: Machines capable of replacing human workforce

By James Day and Oliver Stallwood

Honda's remarkable ASIMO robot during a demonstration at the Tokyo Motor Show.

It was once just a prophecy of Hollywood's wildest sci-fi blockbusters, but a world where robots take charge of everything from law enforcement to schools may soon become reality.

Three Johnny 5-lookalike robot guards are about to clock on for a month-long trial at a South Korean prison. They are trained to look out for the threat of violence and suicide, and experts predict this is the beginning of a society where mankind rubs shoulders with machines.

The 1.5m robots, which cost £553,000, have four wheels and the ability to speak. Kitted out with cameras and sensors, each droid is programmed to analyse sudden unusual behaviour.

The trial will be carried out at the jail in Pohang, south-east of Seoul, from March.

South Korea is keen to blaze a robotic trail, with £415 million spent on research in the sector between 2002 and 2010. But across the world, the hunger for mechanized help is soaring.

A recent study by the International Federation of Robotics revealed 2.2 million service robots for domestic use were sold in 2010, up 35 per cent on 2009. The same report estimates sales of domestic robots could reach more than 9.8 million units between 2011 and 2014.

Dr Stephen Prior, a robotics expert from Middlesex University, says predictions of a world infested with robot servants could finally be here.

But if Hollywood's droid-filled future is being realized, we shouldn't dismiss the fictional foibles of a mechanized world. 'In 50 years, robots could be more intelligent than we are,' warns Dr Prior. 'What happens when it doesn't want to listen? It's like creating a species. You might think you can switch it off but it will know where the switch is.'

Activity 6

Compare the ways in which language is used for effect in the two texts on pages 61–62. Give some examples and analyse what the effects are.

Remember to:

- select some words, phrases or language features from both texts

- analyse the effects of the examples of language that you have selected

- compare the similarities and differences in the use of language in both texts.

Peer-assessment

Activity 7

1. Now swap your response with a partner. Does your partner's response:

    a. select some words, phrases or language features from both texts?

    b. analyse the effects of the examples of language that have been selected?

    c. compare the similarities and differences in the use of language in both texts?

2. Make some notes on what your partner has done successfully and what could be improved.

3. Now spend a few minutes giving your partner some feedback on their work.

Improving your answer

Now read the following example of a complete response to 'Fascination' and 'Rise of the robots: Machines capable of replacing human workforce'. As it stands, it would be placed in Band 3, but the annotations show how you could improve the response by developing parts of it further. This would move it up into Band 4. You would not need to include all of these additions to move into Band 4; they are just examples of the sort of things you could say.

> Compare the ways in which language is used for effect in the two texts. Give some examples and analyse what the effects are.

To move into Band 4 you could add: 'The purpose of Source 3 is to entertain, so the language is mostly positive and facts are used to engage the reader, whereas Source 2 has a warning tone, meaning the facts are used more to scare than to entertain.'

Assessing the response ▶

Band 4: perceptive/detailed

Band 3: clear/relevant ✔

Band 2: some/attempts

Band 1: limited

The writers of Source 3 and Source 2 both use facts but the effects are different. In Source 3, the book Robert Macfarlane is reading has lots of real place names, for example, 'the Far East Rongbuk glacier, the Dzongpen of Shekar, the Lhakpa La'. These places sound very foreign and 'unfamiliar'; the effect of this is to create an air of mystery. The reader can understand why Robert is so in awe because the words sound exotic and exciting. Source 2 also contains facts but they have a negative rather than a positive effect. It uses statistics to explain how the sale of robots is increasing: 'A recent study by the International Federation of Robotics revealed 2.2 million service robots for domestic use were sold in 2010, up 35 per cent on 2009.' This is already a big number but when it then predicts 'more than 9.8 million units between 2011 and 2014' we start to feel scared. It makes it sound as if robots are going to take over the world.

To move into Band 4 you could add: 'This point is strengthened by the use of the word "infested", which suggests mankind is about to be overrun. "Infested" has connotations of pests and viruses, and hints at the damage and destruction so many robots could cause.'

Source 3 is very descriptive and Macfarlane uses lots of similes to show how exciting he thinks the stories are. He says the mountain climbers on Everest had oxygen bottles on their backs which 'made them look like scuba-divers'. Scuba-diving is an extreme sport so this adds to the exotic feeling and we understand why he is so fascinated. He also says they climbed up the North Col 'using ropes and ladders, like medieval warriors besieging a city'. Comparing the mountain to a 'city' conveys how big it is and therefore how brave they were. Source 2 uses metaphors rather than similes; for example, it talks about a society where 'mankind rubs shoulders with machines'. The effect of this is to make us think that robots and humans are going to live together happily.

Both writers use language to show how people can become obsessed with things. In Source 2, it says 'the hunger for mechanized help is soaring'. The word 'soaring' suggests more and more people want to have robots and 'hunger' shows how badly they want them. In Source 3, Robert Macfarlane gets obsessed with the books. He says 'I was carried out of myself' and the effect of this is that the reader can see he is completely involved in the story.

Overall, Source 3 has very positive language, whereas in Source 2 some of the language is negative because the robots come with a warning.

To move into Band 4 you could add: 'The word "besieging" also implies they had to conquer Everest, like they were at war with the mountain and had to fight it until it surrendered. This emphasizes their courage and determination, and makes Robert Macfarlane think they are heroes.'

To move into Band 4 you could add: 'Another way of looking at this phrase, however, is that it suggests equality between humans and robots in the future and this makes the idea more threatening. If robots can become equal, maybe they can also become better.'

To move into Band 4 you could add: 'The phrase almost suggests an out-of-body experience. He is defenceless against the power of the stories and is transported to faraway lands of adventure, which he loves. This is a much more positive obsession than in Source 2, where "hunger" shows that it is a need that must be fulfilled in order to survive.'

Activity 8 | Peer-assessment

Having looked at the student response on pages 64–65, which shows you how to move a Band 3 response up to a Band 4, complete the following tasks:

1. Look again at your own response to 'Fascination' and 'Rise of the robots: Machines capable of replacing human workforce'. With your partner, decide which band your response fits into at the moment. Use the Mark Scheme on page 50 to help you make your decision.

2. Discuss which parts of your response you could develop in order to improve it.

3. Rewrite your response with the parts you developed, and see if you have now achieved a higher mark.

So far, you have learnt how to approach Question 4 by focusing on three key skills:

- selecting
- analysing
- comparing.

Now see how confident you feel that you have understood this approach by completing the self-assessment below.

Self-assessment

1.	I have learnt that I need to select some words, phrases or language features.	Not sure	Confident
2.	I have learnt that I do not have time to select every type of language the writer has used, and that I should just concentrate on the examples that I find most effective.	Not sure	Confident
3.	I have learnt that I need to analyse the language I have selected and explain the effects on the reader of the words, phrases and language features.	Not sure	Confident
4.	I have learnt that I should quote the actual words and phrases that I am analysing.	Not sure	Confident
5.	I have learnt that I need to compare words, phrases or language features in Source 3 and either Source 1 or Source 2.	Not sure	Confident
6.	I have learnt that I have to compare the writers' choice of language and not compare content or structure.	Not sure	Confident

Try it yourself (on your own)

Finally, read the following texts, 'Ennis weighs in with telling response to "fat" critics' by Simon Turnbull (Source 2, page 68) and 'Stephen Fry in America' by Stephen Fry (Source 3, page 69), and write your own complete response to the sample Question 4 task in Activity 9, applying all the key skills you have learnt.

Read the Mark Scheme below before you complete Activity 9. The Mark Scheme will help you to remember what is being assessed.

AO2, i, iii English AO3, i, iii English Language	Skills
Band 4 'perceptive' 'detailed' 13–16 marks	• offers a full and detailed understanding of the texts in relation to language • analyses how the writers have used language to achieve their effects in different contexts • offers appropriate quotations in support of ideas with perceptive comments • focuses on comparison and cross-referencing of language features between the texts
Band 3 'clear' 'relevant' 9–12 marks	• shows clear evidence that the texts are understood in relation to language • offers clear explanation of the effect of words and phrases in the different contexts • offers relevant quotations or references to support ideas • offers clear comparisons and cross references of language features between the two texts

Activity 9

Complete the following sample Question 4 task using the texts on pages 68–69.

> Compare the ways in which language is used for effect in the two texts. Give some examples and analyse what the effects are.

Ennis weighs in with telling response to 'fat' critics

By Simon Turnbull

It was highly debatable whether Jessica Ennis had a weight problem going into her Olympic heptathlon dress rehearsal here in the tranquil western corner of Austria. She certainly has one now.

The weight of expectation on the shoulders of the 8st 13lb slip of a Sheffield lass will not be inconsiderable following the major victory she achieved at the expense of her Olympic rivals in the two-day Hypo-Meeting, the annual early-season contest between the world's best all-round athletes.

The 12-year-old British record was well beaten. It had stood at 6,831 points to Denise Lewis, but having equalled her best ever long-jump mark, set a new javelin personal best and pushed from gun to tape in the 800m yesterday, Ennis finished with a tally of 6,906 points. That put her 75 points ahead of Lewis's record.

No sooner had Ennis picked herself up off the floor after her exhausting effort in the 800m than a

Union Flag was thrust into her hands and she was being asked whether she could emulate Lewis and follow a British record with a gleaming Olympic gold. 'I don't want to even think about that yet,' the 26-year-old replied. 'I just want to enjoy this moment and stay focused. I know that I am in great shape and that I can build on this.'

Asked whether she wanted to put down a decisive pre-Olympic

marker, the beaming new British record holder replied: 'I wanted to do it for me. It gives me the self-belief and the mental capacity going forward.'

It also gives Ennis a place in the record books as the first British athlete to complete a hat-trick of wins here in the spiritual home of multi-events.

While making a series of documentary films about America, Stephen Fry was invited to a Ben and Jerry's factory to create his own ice cream.

Invention

He hands me a white lab coat while I ponder the task before me.

The base, I decide, should be of good vanilla-bean ice cream, nothing more fancy than that. To hand are spatulas, spoons and little pots and bags of semi-frozen ingredients: cookie dough, biscuity substances, chocolate in the shape of a cow and so forth. I try to stay calm. I mustn't be too childish about this, what little dignity I have left is at stake. The temptation to produce a pink confection filled with marshmallows, strawberries and cake mix is strong, but I feel the need to fly the flag for British style and discretion. I find an ingredient called English toffee and swirl it into the vanilla base. Good. Not the kind of hard black toffees Kensington nannies gave children in their prams to keep them quiet while they kissed the footman, but a good start. To this promising base I add chocolate fudge, a gloopy substance that freezes when added to the ice cream, like a lava flow meeting water. A granulated texture is added with which I feel well pleased.

Very fine – strong, adult, not too sweet, but there's something missing … I rootle and scrabble, searching for the magic extra ingredient that will transform my mixture into a true flavour, my rough prototype into a working masterpiece. The clock is ticking, for a tour party is about to come in at any moment and I am to feed them and then stand with bowed head to receive their judgement.

Just as I am about to give up and offer my acceptable but now to my mind rather lame decoction my fingers curl around a bag of knobbly somethings. I have found it! It adds crunch, a hint of sophisticated bitterness and a rich musty, nutty centre around which the other flavours can play their toffee-like, chocolaty games. Walnuts! I stir them in with my spatula and Sean helps me transfer the giant mixture into small tourist-sized tubs. This is done by squeezing a kind of piping bag. Within seconds I have lost all feeling in my hands.

'It's very cold,' I observe.

'Many are cold,' says Sean, 'but few are frozen.'

Before I have time to throw something at him, the tour party enters.

'Welcome everybody,' beams Sean. 'This is a special occasion. You will be trying a new flavour, mixed by our Guest Flavorist, here. His invention is called …?'

'Er … I … that is … um …'

'… is called "Even Stephens"!' extemporizes Sean happily.

I stand meekly, submissively, hopefully while the tourists surge forward to begin the tasting. Despite my humble demeanour, I know, I really know that I have struck gold. There have not been many moments in my life when I have been quite so sure of success. But here, I am convinced, is a perfect blend of flavours.

The tourists agree. Once the filming stops and the camera crew have dived in too there is nothing left of Even Stephens but my memory of a solid-gold vanilla-based triumph.

Stephen, you created an ice-cream flavour. And it was good. Now you may rest.

Preparing for Section B: Writing

What is the content and focus of the exam?

Unit 1 Section B is worth 40 marks. It is where you are the writer and your ability to produce non-fiction texts is assessed. You have to complete two writing tasks: one shorter task worth 16 marks and one longer task worth 24 marks. In the shorter task you have to write to inform/explain/describe and in the longer task you have to write to argue/persuade. You have to demonstrate that you can adapt your style of writing to fit the topic, purpose and audience.

How to use your time in the exam

You should aim to spend 1 hour on the Writing section (having spent 1 hour 15 minutes on the Reading section). The following provides a suggestion for how you could divide up your time in the Writing section of the exam:

Question and word count	Marks available	Suggested timing
Question 5: There is no specified length, but you should aim for approximately 300–350 words for Question 5.	16 marks (10 marks for Communication and Organization of Ideas; 6 marks for Accuracy)	25 minutes (including a few minutes at the start to plan and a few minutes to proofread your answer at the end)
Question 6: There is no specified length, but you should aim for approximately 400–450 words for Question 6.	24 marks (16 marks for Communication and Organization of Ideas; 8 marks for Accuracy)	35 minutes (including a few minutes at the start to plan and a few minutes to proofread your answer at the end)

While both questions test the same skills, you are expected to develop and sustain your ideas more in the longer task. This Writing section is therefore divided into two chapters, with each one focusing on a separate question. It is essential that you attempt both Writing questions in the exam in order to demonstrate all the necessary skills. If you miss out a question, you will not achieve the mark that you want.

Assessment Objectives (AOs)

Assessment Objectives are the skills being assessed during your GCSE course. Below is a table that shows you the AOs that you need to demonstrate in the Writing section of the Unit 1 exam:

AO number	AO wording	Question this AO applies to in Section B: Writing
AO3, i English AO4, i English Language	Write to communicate clearly, effectively and imaginatively, using and adapting forms and selecting vocabulary appropriate to task and purpose in ways that engage the reader.	You need to demonstrate this AO in Question 5 and Question 6 (Communication).
AO3, ii English AO4, ii English Language	Organize information and ideas into structured and sequenced sentences, paragraphs and whole texts, using a variety of linguistic and structural features to support cohesion and overall coherence.	You need to demonstrate this AO in Question 5 and Question 6 (Organization of Ideas).
AO3, iii English AO4, iii English Language	Use a range of sentence structures for clarity, purpose and effect, with accurate punctuation and spelling.	You need to demonstrate this AO in Question 5 and Question 6 (Accuracy).

By working through the Writing chapters of this book, you will practise these key skills and learn exactly where you need to demonstrate them in the exam in order to achieve your best possible mark.

Mark Scheme

Imagine a ladder with four rungs. Each rung represents a band in a Mark Scheme. The examiner uses this Mark Scheme to assess your responses: the bottom rung is Band 1 and the top rung is Band 4.

Each mark band is summed up by a key word or words. For Writing, the key words are:

Band 4: convincing/compelling

Band 3: clarity/success

Band 2: some

Band 1: limited

Each mark band consists of a range of skills, based on the Assessment Objectives above, which students have to demonstrate – the further up the ladder you climb, the more demanding the skills become. The key words and the skills being tested are common to both Writing questions and an extract from the Mark Scheme that examiners use is included in this introduction.

Higher tier students are aiming for Band 3 or Band 4 and this book aims to help you achieve the best mark of which you are capable.

Section B: Writing

Communication and Organization of Ideas

An extract from the Mark Scheme that examiners use to mark Questions 5 and 6 is printed below. For Communication and Organization of Ideas there are four mark bands in total, but Higher tier students are aiming for Band 3 or Band 4. The key words for each band are on the left-hand side and the skills you have to demonstrate in your response are on the right. Notice the differences between Band 3 and Band 4.

AO3, i, ii English AO4, i, ii English Language	Skills
Band 4 'convincing' 'compelling' Question 5: 8–10 marks Question 6: 13–16 marks	**Communication** • communicates in a way which is convincing, and increasingly compelling • form, content and style are consistently matched to purpose and audience, and becoming assuredly matched • engages the reader with structured and developed writing, with an increasingly wide range of integrated and complex details • writes in a formal way, employing a tone that is appropriately serious but also manipulative, subtle and increasingly abstract • uses linguistic devices, such as the rhetorical question, hyperbole, irony and satire, in a consciously crafted way that is increasingly sustained • shows control of extensive vocabulary, with word choices becoming increasingly ambitious **Organization of Ideas** • employs fluently linked paragraphs and seamlessly integrated discursive markers • uses a variety of structural features, for example, different paragraph lengths, indented sections, dialogue, bullet points, in an increasingly inventive way • presents complex ideas in a coherent way
Band 3 'clarity' 'success' Question 5: 5–7 marks Question 6: 9–12 marks	**Communication** • communicates in a way which is clear, and increasingly successful • clear identification with purpose and audience, with form, content and style becoming increasingly matched • engages the reader with a range of material, with writing becoming more detailed and developed • writes in a formal way, employing a tone that is appropriately serious and clearly chosen, with increasing anticipation of reader response • uses linguistic devices, such as the rhetorical question, hyperbole, lists and anecdote, as appropriate, and increasingly to engage and interest the reader • shows evidence of a clear selection of vocabulary for effect, with increasing sophistication in word choice and phrasing **Organization of Ideas** • employs usually coherent paragraphs that are increasingly used to enhance meaning, for example, one-sentence paragraphs, and increasingly integrated discursive markers • uses a variety of structural features, for example, direct address to reader, indented sections, dialogue, bullet points, increasingly effectively • presents well thought-out ideas in sentences

Accuracy

For Accuracy there are three mark bands in total, but Higher tier students are aiming for Band 3 or the top of Band 2. The skills you have to demonstrate in your response are in the right-hand column of the table below. Notice the differences between Band 2 and Band 3.

AO3, iii English AO4, iii English Language	Skills
Band 3 Question 5: 5–6 marks Question 6: 6–8 marks	**Accuracy** • uses complex grammatical structures and punctuation with success • organizes writing using sentence demarcation accurately • employs a variety of sentence forms to good effect including short sentences • shows accuracy in the spelling of words from an ambitious vocabulary • uses Standard English consistently
Band 2 Question 5: 3–4 marks Question 6: 3–5 marks	**Accuracy** • writes with control of agreement, punctuation and sentence construction • organizes writing using sentence demarcation which is mainly accurate • employs a variety of sentence forms • shows accuracy in the spelling of words in common use in an increasingly developed vocabulary • uses Standard English usually

What to expect in the exam

Key term

Inform To tell, to give the main facts or ideas about something or someone.

Explain To give reasons for something: the what, why or how.

Describe To make something come alive by using vivid details and language features.

In the exam, Question 5 is the shorter Writing task and is worth 16 marks. 10 of these marks are awarded for Communication and Organization of Ideas and 6 are for Accuracy.

The focus of Question 5 is writing to **inform/explain/describe**. It is based on personal experience.

The key to success in Question 5 is how effectively you communicate. This is the first bullet point in each mark band (see the Mark Scheme on page 72) and it is the most important skill. The examiner will place your response into a mark band according to how effectively you communicate and then award a mark within that band, based on how well you demonstrate the rest of the skills. The more successfully you demonstrate each skill, the higher your mark will be.

Writing to inform/explain/describe

The focus of Question 5 is writing to inform/explain/describe and you are being asked to address two of these three purposes. This chapter is designed to show you how to approach Question 5 in the exam and the key skills that you need to demonstrate when writing your response. It is divided into two sections:

- Writing to describe and explain
- Writing to inform and explain.

The first section uses a sample question to guide you through the approach and the key skills and, step by step, builds up to a complete response. At each stage, you will practise the approach and the key skills on another question in order to create your own response. The second section shows you how to place a slightly different emphasis on these key skills.

Once you have mastered how to approach the question and apply the skills, you should feel confident about your ability to do the same in the exam.

Section 1: Writing to describe and explain

Approaching the question

Purpose, audience and form

In the exam, you are given the topic you have to write about. From this, you need to identify the purpose, the audience and the form. This will help you to decide what you are going to write and how you are going to write it.

- The purpose is the reason why you are writing. The purpose may be given to you in the question or it may be implied. This section focuses on the two purposes of writing to describe and explain.

- The audience is the person (or people) you are writing for. The audience may be given to you in the question or it may be implied. You may be asked to write, for example, for readers of a newspaper/magazine, listeners of a radio programme or to your local councillor.

- The form is the type of response you are producing. The form will be given to you in the question. You may be asked to write, for example, an article, a leaflet or a blog entry.

The way to identify purpose, audience and form is summarized in the annotations around the sample question below. This sample question will be used to guide you through how to approach writing to describe and explain, and the key skills required.

*This is the **form**. You are being asked to produce an online piece of personal writing.*

*This is the **audience**. You are being asked to write for the readers of your online blog.*

*This is the **purpose**. You are being asked to describe.*

> Write an entry for your online blog, describing a place you hate and explain why you dislike it so much.

*This is the **purpose**. You are being asked to explain.*

Exam tips

- You can address each purpose (to describe and to explain) separately, or you can combine them. Choose the way that suits you best.

- To achieve Band 4, you need to address both purposes, but they do not have to be addressed equally.

- Sometimes students find it useful to remember purpose, audience and form as PAF.

Activity 1

1. Below is another sample question. Copy out the question and identify the purpose, the audience and the form in the same way as on page 75.

Write a brief article for *Real Life* magazine, describing a childhood memory and explaining why it is important to you.

2. Compare your purpose, audience and form with a partner to see if you agree.

Planning your response

Before you start to write your response in the exam, you need to spend a few minutes thinking about what you are going to say and the order in which you are going to say it. Only then can you think about how you are going to write it.

For the sample question on page 75 about a 'place you hate', you first need to decide on the place. Below are some suggestions:

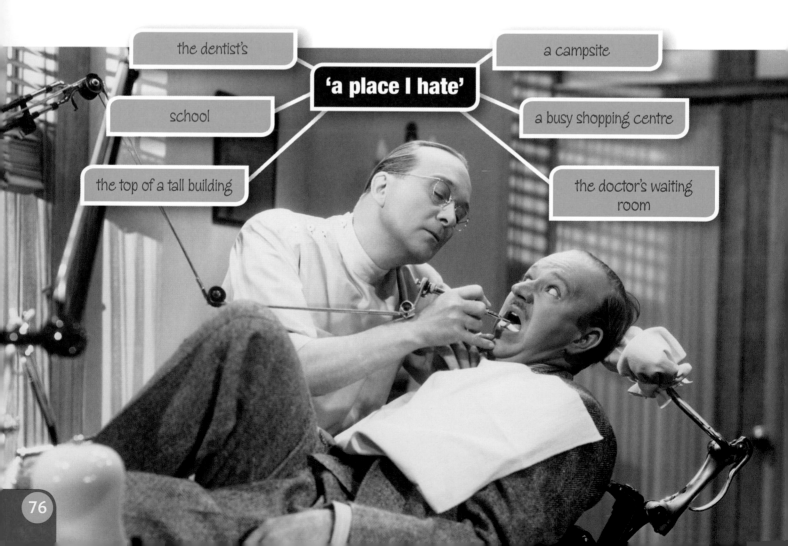

the dentist's

a campsite

'a place I hate'

school

a busy shopping centre

the top of a tall building

the doctor's waiting room

When you have decided on the place, you need to consider what you plan to say about it. Below are some suggestions based on one of the topics opposite:

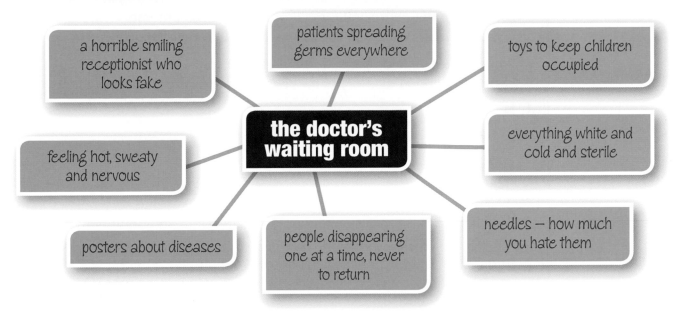

Choosing and using your ideas

The next step is writing your plan. In the exam, you need to decide:

- which of these ideas you are going to use and develop
- how these ideas could be grouped together
- the best order in which to arrange these ideas.

You should focus on four or five main points in your plan and number them. They will form your paragraphs and give your response structure. Make sure you keep your purpose and audience in mind because this will affect your decisions. An example of a plan based on the topic of the doctor's waiting room is included below.

Exam tips

You may want to structure your work in a more adventurous way; for example, using a flashback or introducing a twist at the end. This can be effective but needs to be planned very carefully.

1. Describe the room – posters about diseases on the walls; everything white and cold and sterile; toys to keep children occupied.
2. Describe the receptionist – horrible smiling woman who looks fake.
3. Describe the other patients – spreading germs everywhere; disappearing one at a time, never to return.
4. Describe your own feelings – feeling hot, sweaty and nervous; thinking about needles and how much you hate them.
5. Explain your reasons for disliking this place.

Activity 2

1. Using the example on page 76, draw a spider diagram with 'childhood memory' in the centre and three or four examples of memories around it. Choose the one you think you can write about most effectively.

2. Using the example on page 77, draw another spider diagram with your chosen childhood memory in the centre and add possible ideas around it.

3. Now decide:

   • which of the ideas you are going to use and develop

   • how these ideas could be grouped together

   • the best order in which to arrange these ideas.

4. Write a plan that focuses on four or five main points and number them. These will form your paragraphs and give your response structure. Make sure you keep your purpose and audience in mind because this will affect your decisions.

5. Discuss your plan with a partner and share your ideas. Make a note of any suggestions that improve your plan.

Tone

In the exam, it is important to think about the tone of your response at this stage. Tone means a mood that conveys the writer's attitude. Your tone makes it obvious what you think about the topic or sometimes what you think about the reader. For the sample question on page 75 about a 'place you hate', the tone will be negative because you are writing about something you dislike. In the question about a 'childhood memory' on page 76, your tone might be negative if you are recalling an unhappy memory or nostalgic if you are remembering your childhood in a fond way.

Practising the key skills

The next step is writing your response. This section looks at the key skills that you need to demonstrate and gives you a chance to practise them in order to produce the best non-fiction writing that you can.

Choice of language

To describe means to make something come alive by using vivid details and language features. In the exam, you could be asked to describe many things, such as a person, a place, a time, a feeling or a scene. When writing to describe, you need to use your imagination to create an interesting and engaging picture for your reader. This is done through your choice of language.

Look again at the examples of language listed on page 52 to remind yourself of the types of language a writer could use. In Question 4, you were asked to identify words, phrases and language features in a writer's work and analyse their effect on the reader. Now *you* are the writer and *you* are the one who needs to use words, phrases and language features in order to create an effect.

Exam tips

There are many tones you could adopt, e.g. light-hearted, witty, mocking, bitter, reassuring or angry. You may even vary or adapt your tone throughout your response. The tone you choose is up to you, as long as it is appropriate to your topic, purpose and audience.

Exam tips

- Remember, the focus is on personal experience. You are being asked to apply your imagination to something that has/could have happened. You should not write an imaginative fictional story.

- Sometimes students find it useful to remember language in addition to purpose, audience and form, so PAF becomes PAFL.

Simile A comparison showing the similarity between two quite different things, stating that one is *like* the other, e.g. 'Eating chocolate is *like* going to heaven'.

Metaphor A comparison showing the similarity between two quite different things, stating that one actually *is* the other, e.g. 'When I eat chocolate, I am in heaven'.

Similes and metaphors

When writing to describe, it is important to create a mood or atmosphere so that your reader can experience exactly what it is you are describing. One way of doing this is to include **similes** and **metaphors**.

In your answer to the sample question on page 75 about a 'place you hate', you could include several effective comparisons, for example:

Think about the receptionist in your doctor's surgery. You obviously don't like her, so you want to create an unpleasant effect for your reader. Perhaps she is wearing perfume that is meant to smell lovely but is actually repulsive? What else is meant to have a lovely smell but in reality doesn't? An effective example of a simile here might be to say her perfume is 'like mouldy flowers that have been in a vase for too long'.

Similes and metaphors can be very effective but should not be over-used. They need to fit into your writing naturally and not sound contrived.

Think about the other patients in the waiting room. You've already decided they are spreading germs everywhere, so you want to create an unhealthy effect for your reader. They might be sneezing and coughing and spluttering. What else makes a sneezing, coughing, spluttering sound when it isn't healthy? An effective example of a metaphor here might be to say the patients are 'one big broken engine in a car that won't start'.

Activity 3

1. Using the 'childhood memory' ideas you've already decided on, think of two similes and two metaphors that could be effectively included in your final response. Use your imagination and be as creative and original as possible.

2. Share your ideas with a partner and make a note of any suggestions that could improve your use of simile and metaphor.

Senses

Another way to create mood or atmosphere is to describe what you can see, hear, smell, taste and touch. Most students can describe what they see, but using the other senses helps to create a more complete picture for your reader.

In the sample question on page 75 about a 'place you hate', you have already decided on some senses, but there are others that could be effectively included. The table below shows some examples.

In the sample question on page 75

Senses	Examples
Hear	• other patients sneezing, coughing and spluttering • names being called out to go in to see the doctor • your heart beating fast or the blood pumping in your veins because you're so nervous
Smell	• the receptionist is wearing perfume
Touch	• the waiting room is cold but you feel hot and sweaty • the feeling of the injection needle going into your arm

Exam tips

It is not always appropriate to include all five senses. The senses you choose will depend on what you are describing.

Activity 4

1. Draw a table like the one above. In the column headed 'Senses', list the senses that could be effectively included in your final 'childhood memory' response. In the column headed 'Examples', give two examples for each sense. Use your imagination and be as creative and original as possible.

2. Share your ideas with a partner and make a note of any suggestions that could improve your use of the senses.

Vocabulary choices The deliberate choice of words and phrases to create an effect.

Adjective A word used to describe a person, place or thing, e.g. 'a *sleepy* cat'.

Verb A doing or being word, e.g. 'I *am travelling* to Australia' or 'I *live* here'.

Emotive language Words and phrases deliberately used to provoke an emotional reaction, e.g. 'Missing the concert was *devastating*'.

Exam tips

At all times you need to remember your purpose and audience, and also the tone you have chosen to adopt, because these will determine your vocabulary choices.

Effective vocabulary choices

Another way to create mood or atmosphere is to include effective **vocabulary choices**. The best descriptive writing uses lots of interesting **adjectives** and **verbs**, and sometimes **emotive language** is used to provoke an emotional reaction. The more precise your choice of vocabulary, the greater effect you will have on your reader.

In your answer to the sample question on page 75 about a 'place you hate', there are several effective vocabulary choices that could be included, for example:

Think about the receptionist in your doctor's surgery. You've already decided that she is wearing perfume and that it smells 'like mouldy flowers that have been in a vase for too long'. What would be the best adjective to describe this perfume? 'Nasty' would fit, but doesn't sound quite right. 'Horrible' would fit, but you want to convey to your reader that it is worse than just horrible. An effective vocabulary choice here might be 'disgusting', which sums up for the reader just how unpleasant the smell is.

Think about the other patients in the waiting room. You've already decided that they are 'sneezing and coughing and spluttering, one big broken engine in a car that won't start', but how are they positioned in the room? What would be the best verb to describe them? 'Sitting' would fit, but you want to convey that they are ill and don't really want to be there. An effective vocabulary choice here might be 'slumped', which sums up for the reader just how unhealthy and uninterested they are.

Think about the main reason why you dislike the doctor's surgery: the injection. You've already imagined how the needle feels as it goes into your arm. What would be the best example of emotive language to describe the pain? 'Bad' would fit, but it's too ordinary. 'Dreadful' would fit, but you want to communicate to your reader that it is worse than that. An effective vocabulary choice here might be 'excruciating', which sums up for the reader just how extremely painful it is.

Activity 5

1. Using the 'childhood memory' ideas that you've already decided on, list three adjectives, three verbs and three examples of emotive language that could be effectively included in your final response. Use your imagination and be as creative and original as possible.

2. Share your ideas with a partner and make a note of any suggestions that could improve your vocabulary choices.

Key term

Rhetorical question A question asked to make a point where no answer is expected.

Alliteration The deliberate repetition of the same sound at the beginning of words to create an effect, e.g. '*crawling crabs*'.

Pattern of three Listing three things to create a specific effect, e.g. 'To pass your exam you need *a pen*, *a piece of paper* and *a brain*'.

Other language features

You can also create mood or atmosphere by including some of the other language features listed on page 52.

In your answer to the sample question on page 75 about a 'place you hate', there are several other language features that could be effectively included, for example:

Talking directly to the reader would be effective because you are writing a blog – a regular, online piece of personal writing, which means your readers are likely to be familiar. You've already decided there are lots of posters about diseases on the walls of the waiting room, which presumably are designed to be informative and interesting, but in reality would just scare patients. What **rhetorical question** would both convey your attitude towards this and engage your reader at the same time? An effective example of a rhetorical question here might be 'Surely they should be trying to reassure people, not make them feel worse?'

Alliteration would draw attention to a particular part of your response and add to your reader's understanding and enjoyment. You've already decided that you don't like the receptionist, so perhaps she makes everything around her unpleasant as well. Maybe she is sitting in a corner at an old desk. What other words beginning with 'd' (to go with 'desk') could you use to create a dull, miserable sound? An effective example here might be 'sitting behind a dark, depressing desk'.

A **pattern of three** would also draw attention to a particular part of your response and add to your reader's understanding and enjoyment. An effective example of a pattern of three here might be 'The waiting room walls are white, cold and sterile'.

Activity 6

1. Using the 'childhood memory' ideas that you've already decided on, look again at the language features listed on page 52 and choose three that have not already been used.

   Think of one example of each that could be effectively included in your final response. Think of the effect you are trying to create for your reader and how to do this using these language features. Use your imagination and be as creative and original as possible.

2. Share your ideas with a partner and make a note of any suggestions that could improve your use of selected language features.

Exam tips

As with similes and metaphors, it is important not to over-use these language features. They need to fit into your writing naturally and not sound contrived.

Openings

In order to interest your reader immediately, it is essential to write an engaging opening. The opening paragraph, especially the first sentence, is crucial.

In the sample question on page 75 about a 'place you hate', you have already decided on the content of your opening paragraph in your plan:

> 1. Describe the room – posters about diseases on the walls; everything white and cold and sterile; toys to keep children occupied.

Now you need to decide on the most effective way of writing an opening paragraph that starts with an interesting and engaging first sentence and includes any similes, metaphors, senses, vocabulary choices or other language features that are relevant at this stage. The example on page 86 is annotated to show you how these key skills can be applied. It is taken from a Band 3 response.

> Write an entry for your online blog, describing a place you hate and explain why you dislike it so much.

interesting and engaging first sentence

Student A

The pictures on the walls look deadly. I hate the doctor's surgery, especially the waiting room. The walls are covered with frightening posters full of information about deadly diseases and this creates a scary atmosphere. Surely they should be trying to reassure people, not make them feel worse? The waiting room walls are white, cold and sterile. Horrible.

pattern of three   *rhetorical question*

Exam tips

Notice that the idea about the toys to keep children occupied has not been included in the above opening paragraph after all. This is because it sounds more effective to end with the description of the walls and the one word sentence. Plans are there to guide you, but can be adapted at any time.

Sentences

Notice the different sentence types that are used in Student A's opening paragraph. Varying your sentence structure is another way to make your response interesting and engaging. There are four main types of sentence:

1. A simple sentence has a subject and a main verb, for example:

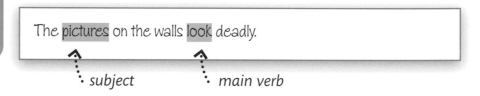

The pictures on the walls look deadly.

subject   main verb

2. A compound sentence is where two or more simple sentences are joined together to make one longer sentence, for example:

first simple sentence

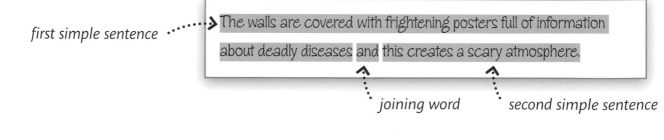

The walls are covered with frightening posters full of information about deadly diseases and this creates a scary atmosphere.

joining word   second simple sentence

3. A complex sentence is where one part of a sentence is dependent on the other, for example:

The word 'especially' leads into the second part of the sentence, which would not make sense without the first part.

I hate the doctor's surgery, especially the waiting room.

4. A minor sentence consists of very few words used deliberately to create an effect, for example:

Horrible.

Sentences with one or two words can be effective, but they should not be over-used.

Activity 7

1. Using your 'childhood memory' plan and the ideas you've already decided on, write your opening paragraph. Think of a first sentence that will interest and engage your reader immediately, and make sure you vary your sentences.

2. Share your opening paragraph with a partner and make a note of any suggestions that could improve it.

Paragraphs

Paragraphs are important because they help you to organize your ideas and make your response easy to follow. All writing needs an opening paragraph to introduce the topic, a final paragraph to conclude and several paragraphs in between.

There are three main ways to paragraph your response effectively:

1. Make sure you start a new paragraph in the right place. The main places where you need to start a new paragraph are:

   ● when you change the subject

   ● when you change the place

   ● when you change the time

   ● when you change the speaker.

   Look again at the plan on page 77. You will see that a new paragraph is started each time the subject changes.

2. Start each paragraph with a **topic sentence** that summarizes the ideas that follow.

3. Make sure your paragraphs are linked. Each one needs to build on the previous one in order to make your response flow.

Key term

Topic sentence A topic sentence is the first sentence of a paragraph and identifies the main idea.

A complete sample response

Now read the following complete response by Student A. It follows the original plan and is annotated to show you how similes, metaphors, senses, vocabulary choices and other language features could be effectively included. This response would be placed at the top of Band 3 as it includes so many of the key skills.

Assessing the response ⬇

Band 4: convincing/compelling

Band 3: clarity/success ✓

Band 2: some

Band 1: limited

> Write an entry for your online blog, describing a place you hate and explain why you dislike it so much.

interesting and engaging first sentence

rhetorical question

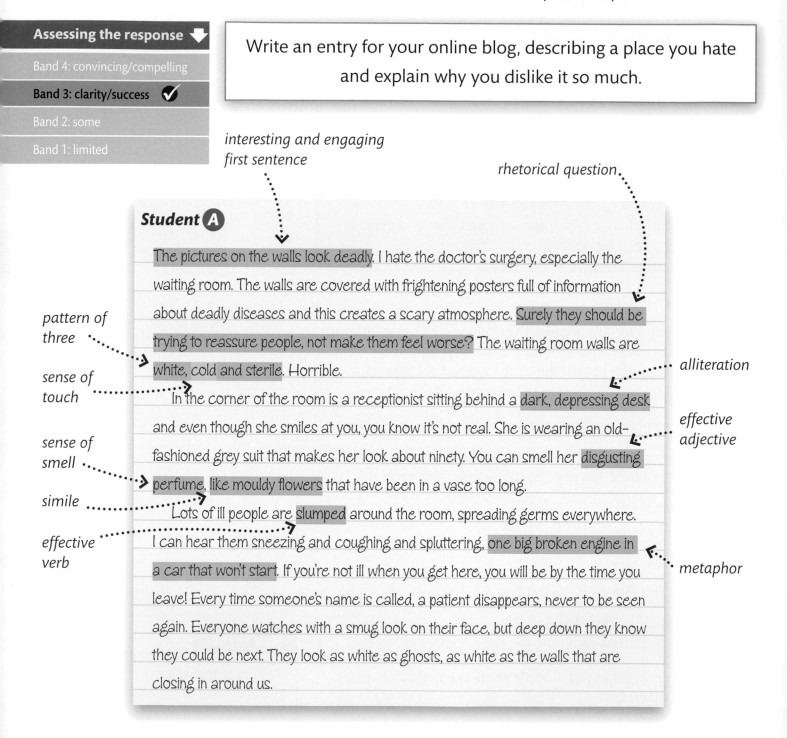

pattern of three

sense of touch

sense of smell

simile

effective verb

alliteration

effective adjective

metaphor

Student A

The pictures on the walls look deadly. I hate the doctor's surgery, especially the waiting room. The walls are covered with frightening posters full of information about deadly diseases and this creates a scary atmosphere. Surely they should be trying to reassure people, not make them feel worse? The waiting room walls are white, cold and sterile. Horrible.

In the corner of the room is a receptionist sitting behind a dark, depressing desk and even though she smiles at you, you know it's not real. She is wearing an old-fashioned grey suit that makes her look about ninety. You can smell her disgusting perfume, like mouldy flowers that have been in a vase too long.

Lots of ill people are slumped around the room, spreading germs everywhere. I can hear them sneezing and coughing and spluttering, one big broken engine in a car that won't start. If you're not ill when you get here, you will be by the time you leave! Every time someone's name is called, a patient disappears, never to be seen again. Everyone watches with a smug look on their face, but deep down they know they could be next. They look as white as ghosts, as white as the walls that are closing in around us.

I'm probably white as well. I feel really sick, even though I'm only here for an injection. The only thing I can think about is the agonizing feeling of the needle *← ·········· sense of touch* going into my arm. In my mind it's as big as a javelin. I get hot and sweaty, and I'm so nervous I can hardly breathe. All I can hear is the blood pumping through my veins *← ······· sense of hearing* and I almost miss my turn when my name is called.

These are the reasons that I hate the doctor's surgery — the waiting room, the receptionist, the patients and the needles. Especially the needles. I try to think of something else, anything else, to take my mind off what is about to happen and the excruciating pain I know I will feel, but I fail miserably. This is the place I hate most. What's yours?

emotive language

Exam tips

- Like the opening sentence, the final sentence needs to have an impact on the reader, as well as rounding off your topic.

- Writing to explain: In the response above, the final paragraph deals with the 'explain' part of the question. The reasons for disliking the doctor's waiting room are implied throughout the response, but also clearly stated at the end.

Try it yourself (with support)

Writing your own complete response

Now you are going to put all the key skills into practice in a complete response to Question 5. You'll be given some support to help you.

Look back over pages 75–89 to remind yourself of how to approach writing to describe and explain.

Activity 8

> Write a brief article for *Real Life* magazine, describing a childhood memory and explaining why it is important to you.

Remember to:

- use your plan
- start with an interesting and engaging first sentence
- start with the opening paragraph you have already written
- include your similes and metaphors, senses, effective vocabulary choices and other language features in the appropriate places
- vary your sentences
- use paragraphs correctly.

Assessing and improving

Look again at the Mark Scheme on pages 72–73. When you have written your response, you need finally to check the accuracy of your work. In the exam, you should allow a few minutes at the end to read through carefully what you have written, checking for any mistakes in spelling, punctuation and grammar.

Activity 9 — Peer-assessment

1. Now swap your response with a partner. Does your partner's response:

   a. start with an interesting and engaging first sentence?

   b. include similes, metaphors, senses, effective vocabulary choices and other language features in appropriate places?

   c. use a varied range of sentences?

   d. use paragraphs correctly?

   e. use spelling, punctuation and grammar accurately? For example, check:

      • spelling – have they confused words that sound the same but are spelt differently, such as 'there/their/they're'?

      • punctuation – have they separated sentences using commas when they should have used full stops?

      • grammar – have they confused singular and plural verbs, such as 'we was' instead of 'we were'?

2. Make some notes on what your partner has done successfully and what could be improved.

3. Now spend a few minutes giving your partner some feedback on their work.

Exam tips

Remember, how effectively you communicate is the most important skill. If you make too many mistakes in spelling, punctuation and grammar, you will not be able to communicate your ideas effectively.

Now read the complete response below by Student B. It follows a similar plan to Student A's and also includes similes and metaphors, senses, effective vocabulary choices and other language features. It would be placed in Band 4.

> Write an entry for your online blog, describing a place you hate and explain why you dislike it so much.

Assessing the response ➡

Band 4: convincing/compelling ✅

Band 3: clarity/success

Band 2: some

Band 1: limited

Student B

On the walls I see death. Plastered on, sneering at me as I enter the surgery: flu, diabetes, meningitis, cancer. The posters are hung like a bad omen, promising evil. The walls are white, the same colour as me. Everything about this place is cold and sterile and I hate it. We all have places we hate and this is mine.

As I walk up to the desk, dread sinks like lead in my belly. There's a receptionist, a simpering woman with a façade of pearls and pink. It's all show. You know the sort I mean, completely fake, like the plastic playhouse in the corner to keep children occupied. The nearer I get, the more I can smell her perfume, a sickly stench that makes me choke, and for a second I think I'm facing death. This place does that to you and this woman doesn't help.

I sit on a plastic, unfeeling chair and look around me at the others. They look so sad, just sitting there waiting for the inevitable. One by one they're called in to see the doctor, panic in their eyes. The ones left behind look grey, as if the souls are seeping out of them. The waiting room is feeding on their life force.

I hold on to the sides of my chair and my knuckles go white. You can't possibly imagine how much I hate everything about this place. All I can think about is the agony I'm about to face. I visualize the metal cabinet where the needles are kept and the thought of it makes me sick. Those needles want me! Blood roars through my veins so fast I can hear it and I hardly notice when my name is called.

I hate needles and I hate the doctor's waiting room. While the receptionist is chatting away in the background, I think about anything to take my mind off what's about to happen. It's useless. That needle is waiting to tear at my skin. Everything about this place is cold and compassionless, and I hate it above all others. I am doomed.

Activity 10

In groups of four, re-read the two student responses (pages 88–89 and opposite) and discuss what Student B does that Student A doesn't. To get you started, you could compare:

1. the opening sentences

2. the use of similes and metaphors

3. the use of senses

4. vocabulary choices

5. the use of other language features

6. sentence variety

7. paragraphs. For example, in Student A's response:

- the third paragraph that starts 'Lots of ill people' lets the reader know that most of the ideas about the patients are going to be contained within that paragraph.

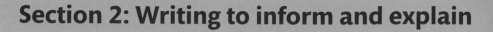

Section 2: Writing to inform and explain

In some ways, writing to inform and explain is very similar to writing to describe and explain. They are both based on personal details and/or experience and the way to approach the question in the exam is identical. However, the key skills that you need to demonstrate in your response have a slightly different emphasis.

To begin with, remind yourself how to approach the question by referring back to pages 75–93.

Exam tips

You are being asked to write the text of a leaflet. You do not need to consider any presentational features.

Activity 11

1. Copy out the sample question below and identify its purpose, audience and form.

> Write the text of a leaflet informing parents of the best ways to deal with difficult children and explaining why these methods work.

2. Draw a spider diagram with 'ways to deal with difficult children' in the centre and write your ideas around this. One idea might be 'keep your child occupied so that they don't become bored and misbehave'.

3. Select the three ideas you think you can write about most effectively.

4. Write a plan that starts with an introduction, ends with a conclusion and includes your chosen three ways of dealing with difficult children.

5. Decide on the tone you want to adopt.

6. Discuss your plan with a partner and share your ideas. Make a note of any suggestions that improve your plan.

Practising the key skills

To inform means to tell, to give the main facts or ideas about something or someone. The best way to interest your reader when writing to inform is by presenting the information in a lively and entertaining way. This is achieved through your choice of language.

Read Student A's complete response opposite. This response would be placed at the top of Band 3 as it includes so many of the key skills.

Write the text of a leaflet informing parents of the best ways to deal with difficult children and explaining why these methods work.

Student A

Is your child's behaviour driving you mad? If so, then this is the guide for you. We all know little kids can be hard work. Some parents face a real battle when their child is naughty and this can affect the whole family. If this sounds like you, read on to find some answers.

The first way to deal with difficult children is to reward them when they do something right. Parents always shout when their kids draw on the wallpaper or spill the orange juice, but sometimes they forget to say well done when their child is good. You could even have a star chart where the stars count towards a bar of chocolate or a day out. The advantage of this method is that your angry, difficult, rebellious child will enjoy being praised rather than just being shouted at and, with a bit of luck, this will make them want to behave.

If this doesn't work, another way of dealing with difficult children is for them to have time out. They use this idea in TV programmes like 'Supernanny', where they make children sit on the naughty step. It is harder than it looks because your child won't want to do it, but you shouldn't give in to their crying. Studies published by Child Life show that this method works as your child has time to think about what they have done wrong. It also shows them there are consequences when you break rules, which is a good thing to learn in life.

Finally, a really good way to stop your child misbehaving is to make sure you spend time with them. Children are like fizzy bottles of lemonade, they need to be dealt with before they explode. Even if you just take them to the park they will know they are getting your attention and therefore won't play up. The more attention you give them and the more activities you do with them, the better they will be.

So if things are bad and you feel like you're losing the battle, why not give these methods a go? I'm sure they will work.

Assessing the response

Band 4: convincing/compelling

Band 3: clarity/success ✓

Band 2: some

Band 1: limited

Exam tips

Writing to explain: In Student A's response the 'explain' part of the question is dealt with in each paragraph. The reasons why the methods work are discussed at the same time as informing the reader of the different ways of dealing with difficult children.

Activity 12

Once you have read Student A's response, re-read 'Selecting language' on page 51.

1. Look at the sentence 'We all know little kids can be hard work'. This is an example of direct address.
   a. Find three examples where 'you' is used to address the reader.
   b. Why is it effective to use 'we' or 'you' when writing to inform?

2. Rhetorical questions have also been used to address the reader directly.
   a. Find two examples in the response on page 95.
   b. Why is it effective to use rhetorical questions when writing to inform?

3. a. Identify three opinions and one **fact** in Student A's response.
   b. Why is it effective to use **opinions** and facts when writing to inform?

4. Look at the phrase 'some parents face a real battle'. This is an example of a metaphor.
   a. Find an example of a simile in Student A's response.
   b. Why is it effective to use similes and metaphors when writing to inform?

5. Identify any other language features used in Student A's response and explain why they are effective when writing to inform.

6. Discuss your answers with a partner and share your ideas.

7. With your partner, compare the use of language features when writing to inform with how they are used when writing to describe. What are the similarities and differences?

Key term

Fact Something that you can prove is true, e.g. 'Star Trek is a television programme'.

Opinion Something that you believe to be true but may not be, e.g. 'Star Trek is a great television programme'.

Now read Student B's complete response opposite. It follows the same plan as Student A and includes similar language features. It would be placed in Band 4.

Activity 13

In groups of four, discuss what Student B does that Student A doesn't. To get you started, you could compare:

1. the first and final sentences

2. the chosen tone

3. the use of language features

4. the use of paragraphs

5. the variety of sentences.

Write the text of a leaflet informing parents of the best ways to deal with difficult children and explaining why these methods work.

Student **B**

OK, so the all-important childhood years of temper tantrums have arrived. How you deal with your precious offspring at this stage will determine whether your child is going to be the devil in disguise or a perfect angel. It's the ultimate battle of wills and it's essential that you come out on top. This guide is designed to help you through these troublesome times.

The first method of dealing with your difficult child? Willpower. Willpower isn't just refraining from having that chocolate bar or sticking it out at the gym. Willpower is saying no to your toddler so that they learn they can't always have what they want, when they want it. Remember Veruca Salt from 'Charlie and the Chocolate Factory'? Look what happened to her! It is never a good idea to spoil children. Next time your child picks up a packet of sweets, say no. When they have a tantrum about it, ignore them. In a child's mind a tantrum equals attention and attention equals a reward. Make 'no' your favourite word in the dictionary. Have willpower. Be strong.

Another way to deal with difficult children is productivity. Keep them occupied. Bored children are difficult children. Without something to do they are pocket rockets, ready to explode. Starting a project, or even better, a game outdoors, can work because it creates a physical outlet for all that energy they generate. It may even tire them out just long enough for you to get a wink of sleep, a reward for all your hard parenting work.

And talking of rewards ... children like to work for things. It builds character and there's always more motivation if there's something to gain. If you want your child to do something or behave in a certain way, give them an incentive (although you do need to choose your rewards wisely — if you bribe them with sweets packed with e-numbers, this method will backfire!).

So there you have it, a crash course in dealing with difficult offspring. You can't sail through this stage with nothing but hope. Follow these practical steps and you should emerge victorious.

Try it yourself (with support)

Writing your own complete response

Now you are going to put all the key skills into practice in a complete response to another Question 5 task.

Look back over pages 94–97 to remind yourself of how to approach writing to inform and explain.

Activity 14

1. Write a brief article for the entertainment section of your local newspaper, informing readers about your favourite singer or band, and explain the reasons for your choice.

2. Check your response and correct any mistakes in spelling, punctuation and grammar.

So far, you have learnt how to approach Question 5 by focusing on two things:

- what to do before you start to write your response
- what key skills to include in your response.

Now see how confident you feel that you have understood this approach by completing the self-assessment opposite.

Self-assessment

1.	I have learnt that the topic I have to write about is given to me in the question and I need to identify the purpose, audience and form.	Not sure	Confident
2.	I have learnt that before I start to write my response, I need to think of ideas and then write a plan.	Not sure	Confident
3.	I have learnt that I need to think about tone before I start to write my response.	Not sure	Confident
4.	I have learnt that how effectively I communicate is the most important skill.	Not sure	Confident
5.	I have learnt that when writing to describe and explain, I need to include similes and metaphors, senses, effective vocabulary choices and other relevant language features.	Not sure	Confident
6.	I have learnt that when writing to inform and explain, I need to emphasize slightly different language features from when writing to describe.	Not sure	Confident
7.	I have learnt that I need to start with an effective opening and that my first sentence is crucial.	Not sure	Confident
8.	I have learnt that I need to vary my sentence structure.	Not sure	Confident
9.	I have learnt that I need to organize my response into paragraphs and link them effectively.	Not sure	Confident
10.	I have learnt that I need to check the accuracy of my work for spelling, punctuation and grammar mistakes when I finish writing.	Not sure	Confident

Try it yourself (on your own)

Write a complete response to each of the following tasks:

> Write a brief article for a website of your choice, describing a situation when you, or someone you know, felt under pressure, and explain how the situation was resolved.

> Your school or college has been given £20,000 by a local sponsor in order to make improvements. Write a letter to the sponsor, informing him or her of how the money will be used and explaining how it will help to raise standards.

Exam tips

If you are asked to write a letter in the exam, do not include an address but begin with 'Dear ...' and sign off appropriately. If you begin 'Dear Madam' or 'Dear Sir', end with 'Yours faithfully'. If you begin with a person's name, for example, 'Dear Mr Cameron', end with 'Yours sincerely'.

What to expect in the exam

In the exam, Question 6 is the longer Writing task and is worth 24 marks. 16 of these marks are awarded for Communication and Organization of Ideas and 8 are for Accuracy.

The focus of Question 6 is writing to **argue/persuade**. You are being asked to adopt a point of view and sustain and develop it.

The key to success in Question 6 is how effectively you communicate. This is the first bullet point in each mark band (see Mark Scheme on page 72) and it is the most important skill. The examiner will place your response into a mark band according to how effectively you communicate and then award a mark within that band, based on how well you demonstrate the rest of the skills. The more successfully you demonstrate each skill, the higher your mark will be.

Writing to argue/persuade

The focus of Question 6 is writing to argue/persuade and you are being asked to address one of these two purposes. This chapter is designed to show you how to approach Question 6 in the exam and the key skills that you need to demonstrate when writing your response. It is divided into two sections:

- Writing to argue
- Writing to persuade.

The first section uses a sample question to guide you through the approach and the key skills and, step by step, builds up to a complete response. At each stage, you will practise the approach and the key skills on another question in order to create your own response. The second section shows you how to place a slightly different emphasis on these key skills.

Once you have mastered how to approach the question and apply the skills, you should feel confident about your ability to do the same in the exam.

Section 1: Writing to argue

Approaching the question

Purpose, audience and form

In the exam, you are given the topic you have to write about. From this, you need to identify the purpose, the audience and the form. This will help you to decide what you are going to write and how you are going to write it.

- The purpose is the reason why you are writing. The purpose may be given to you in the question or it may be implied. This section focuses on the purpose of writing to argue.

- The audience is the person (or people) you are writing for. The audience may be given to you in the question or it may be implied. You may be asked to write, for example, for readers of a newspaper/magazine, listeners of a radio programme or to your local councillor.

- The form is the type of response you are producing. The form will be given to you in the question. You may be asked to write, for example, an article, a leaflet or a blog entry.

The way to identify purpose, audience and form is summarized in the annotations around the sample question below. This sample question will be used to guide you through how to approach writing to argue and the key skills required.

*This is the **form**. You are being asked to produce an article for a magazine of your choice.*

> 'Celebrities exploit their position in society and offer nothing in return.' Write an article for a magazine of your choice, arguing for or against this idea.

*This is the **purpose**. You are being asked to argue your point of view.*

*This is the **audience**. You are being asked to write for the readers of your chosen magazine.*

Activity 1

1. Below is another sample question. Copy out the question and identify the purpose, the audience and the form in the same way as on page 101.

> Many people believe that it is our duty to support space exploration, whatever the cost. Write an article for a website which argues for or against the idea of exploring other worlds.

2. Compare your purpose, audience and form with a partner to see if you agree.

Exam tips

There is no right or wrong answer to Question 6. The point of view you choose to adopt is up to you.

Planning your response

Before you start to write your response in the exam, you need to spend a few minutes thinking about what you are going to say and the order in which you are going to say it. Only then can you think about how you are going to write it.

For the sample question on page 101 about 'celebrities', you first need to decide on the point of view you are going to adopt. You may completely agree with the statement, completely disagree with it or agree with just parts of it. It is important to have a clearly defined point of view so that you can argue your case convincingly.

When you have decided on your point of view, you need to think about some of the reasons why you believe it to be true. You should also consider some of the reasons why it may not be true. Below are some possible arguments both for and against the statement.

everyone thinks they can be a celeb

some are rich but don't actually do anything

make kids want to be famous

bad role models by getting drunk and having affairs

'celebrities'

fake tans and designer clothes

inspire us

many have no talent

charity work

reality TV makes celebs out of wannabes

some talented singers and film stars

Choosing and using your reasons

The next step is writing your plan. In the exam, you need to decide:

- which of the reasons you are going to use and develop
- how these reasons could be grouped together
- the best order in which to arrange these reasons.

This is a crucial stage when writing to argue. How you structure your argument determines how convincing it will be. It should consist of three parts:

- The first part: it is important to state your point of view clearly at the beginning of your response so that everything follows on logically from it.
- The middle part: in addition to developing and sustaining your own point of view, it is important to include the other side of the argument. This will show that you have considered it and dismissed it because your point of view is stronger.
- The final part: it is important to conclude your response by summing up your points, referring back to the title and re-stating your point of view.

There are several ways you can structure the middle part of your argument. The most effective is to present your counter-argument first, dismiss it and then develop and sustain your side of the argument. This ensures that your reader engages more with your point of view.

You should focus on four or five main points in your plan and number them. These will form your paragraphs and give your response structure. Make sure you keep your purpose and audience in mind because this will affect the decisions that you make. An example of a plan based on mainly agreeing with the statement that 'celebrities exploit their position in society and offer nothing in return' is included below.

Exam tips

You could choose to combine your argument and counter-argument throughout your response, but this is a more challenging approach.

1. Introduction — comment on the position of celebrities in society; say you mostly agree with the statement.

2. Counter-argument — some talented singers and film stars; charity work; inspire us.

3. Your point of view — many have no talent; some are rich but don't actually do anything; fake tans and designer clothes.

4. Development of your point of view — bad role models by getting drunk and having affairs.

5. Conclusion.

Activity 2

Based on the question about 'exploring other worlds' on page 102, complete the following tasks:

1. Decide whether you completely agree with the statement, completely disagree with the statement or agree with just parts of it.

2. Using the example on page 102, draw a spider diagram with 'space exploration' in the centre and some arguments for and against the statement around it.

3. Now decide:

   • which of the reasons you are going to use and develop

   • how these reasons could be grouped together

   • the best order in which to arrange these reasons.

4. Write a plan that focuses on four or five main points and number them. These will form your paragraphs and give your response structure. Make sure you keep your purpose and audience in mind because this will affect your decisions.

5. Discuss your plan with a partner and share your ideas. Make a note of any suggestions that improve your plan.

Exam tips

There are many tones you could adopt, e.g. light-hearted, witty, mocking, bitter, reassuring or angry. You may even vary or adapt your tone throughout your response. The tone you choose is up to you, as long as it is appropriate to your topic, purpose and audience.

Key term

Irony Saying the opposite of what you mean in order to make a point, e.g. 'I just love it when the Internet crashes'.

Tone

In the exam, it is important to think about the tone of your response at this stage. Tone means a mood that conveys the writer's attitude. Your tone makes it obvious what you think about the topic or sometimes what you think about the reader. For the sample question on page 101 about 'celebrities', the tone will depend on the point of view you adopt. Having decided that you mostly agree with the statement, your tone could be sarcastic, annoyed or **ironic**.

In your response to the question about 'exploring other worlds', your tone could be disbelieving, enthusiastic or cautious, depending on the point of view you decide to adopt.

Practising the key skills

The next step is writing your response. This section looks at the key skills that you need to demonstrate and gives you a chance to practise them in order to produce the best non-fiction writing that you can.

Choice of language

To argue means to convince someone to have the same point of view as you. In the exam, you are given a controversial statement that has been deliberately chosen because it provokes many different, strongly held **opinions**. When writing to argue, you need to draw your reader in to the argument and prove to them that your opinion is the one they should hold. In addition to the tone you choose to adopt, this is done through your choice of language.

Look again at the examples of language listed on page 52 to remind yourself of the types of language a writer could use. In Question 4, you were asked to identify words, phrases and language features in a writer's work and analyse their effect on the reader. Now *you* are the writer and *you* are the one who needs to use words, phrases and language features in order to create an effect.

Evidence

When writing to argue, it is important to convince your reader. One way of doing this is to provide evidence to support what you are saying. Evidence includes the opinions of others who hold the same point of view, especially experts on the topic, **facts** (and sometimes opinions presented as facts) and **statistics**, examples and **anecdotes**.

Key term

Opinion Something that you believe to be true but may not be, e.g. '*Star Trek* is a great television programme'.

Fact Something that you can prove is true, e.g. '*Star Trek* is a television programme'.

Statistics Numbers and figures, e.g. '*Twenty thousand* people answered the survey'.

Anecdote A short, personal story about something interesting that has happened.

Exam tips

- Presenting an opinion as if it is a fact suggests that there is no room for disagreement, e.g. 'It's obvious that size zero models are too thin'.

- To achieve Band 4, you need to reflect on the wider, more abstract implications of a topic, such as the moral or social considerations, in addition to including concrete evidence.

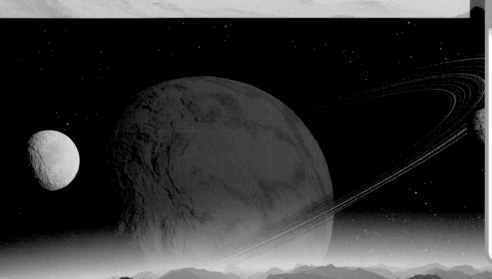

Exam tips

Because you are unlikely to have specialized knowledge about the topic in the exam, you are allowed to invent your own 'experts' and 'facts', but you need to make sure what you claim is believable.

In your answer to the sample question on page 101 about 'celebrities', you could include several effective types of evidence, for example:

Part of your counter-argument is that some celebrities do charity work. Think of a celebrity who has helped to raise money for good causes. You could mention Angelina Jolie, as it is a documented fact that she has travelled the world to help the poor and has even adopted orphaned children to give them a better life. An effective example of a fact here would be: 'Angelina Jolie does lots of work for charity, as well as adopting children from developing countries'.

As most of your argument is agreeing with the statement, think of the type of celebrity who exploits their position. Perhaps you could include reality TV stars, especially famous families where the children get to experience exciting things just because of their parents. An effective example would be to say that they 'get to do glamorous things like creating their own perfume or presenting the MTV awards, all because they have a father who is extremely rich and once made a TV show'.

Think about the lifestyle lived by celebrities and how this influences what children want to be when they grow up. Perhaps you could include an anecdote to explain that this never used to be the case. An effective example of an anecdote would be: 'children used to dream about growing up to be a fireman or a doctor, but these days they just want to be famous'.

Activity 3

1. Using the 'exploring other worlds' ideas you've already decided on, think of evidence that could be effectively included in your final response. Think of how to convince your reader, using the opinions of others who hold the same point of view, especially experts on the topic, facts (or opinions presented as facts), statistics, examples and anecdotes.

2. Share your ideas with a partner and make a note of any suggestions that could improve your use of evidence.

Effective vocabulary choices

Another way of convincing your reader is to include effective **vocabulary choices**. The best arguments have plenty of strong **adjectives** and **verbs**, and **emotive language** is often used to provoke an emotional reaction. The most effective vocabulary choices also convey the tone you have chosen to adopt. The more precise your choice of vocabulary, the greater the impression you will make on your reader.

In your answer to the sample question on page 101 about 'celebrities', you could include several effective vocabulary choices, for example:

Think about why celebrities offer nothing to society. You've already decided that many of them have no talent. Perhaps you could develop this by saying they don't seem very intelligent, either. An effective adjective to convey this might be 'brainless', which sums up for the reader just how stupid they appear to be and also conveys your attitude.

Think about how some celebrities look. You've already decided that they have fake tans and designer clothes, but you could develop this by saying that these seem to make them think they're better than the rest of us. An effective verb to convey this might be 'flaunting', which sums up for the reader just how superior they appear to feel and also conveys your attitude.

Think about the behaviour of some celebrities. You've already decided they are not good role models because they get drunk and have affairs. An effective example of emotive language here might be 'disgusting', which sums up for the reader just how appalling the behaviour is and also conveys your attitude.

Key term

Vocabulary choices The deliberate choice of words and phrases to create an effect.

Adjective A word used to describe a person, place or thing, e.g. 'a *sleepy* cat'.

Verb A doing or being word, e.g. 'I *am travelling* to Australia' or 'I *live* here'.

Emotive language Words and phrases deliberately used to provoke an emotional reaction, e.g. 'Missing the concert was *devastating*'.

Activity 4

1. Using the 'exploring other worlds' ideas you've already decided on, list three adjectives, three verbs and three examples of emotive language that could be effectively included in your final response. Think of how to convince your reader and convey your attitude using effective vocabulary choices.

2. Share your ideas with a partner and make a note of any suggestions that could improve your vocabulary choices.

Exam tips

These language features can be very effective but should not be over-used. They need to fit into your writing naturally and not sound contrived.

Other language features

Another way to convince your reader is by including some of the other language features listed on page 52.

In your answer to the sample question on page 101 about 'celebrities', there are several other language features that could be effectively included, for example:

Talking directly to the reader would draw them into the argument. One way of doing this is to use words like 'we' and 'us', because this makes the assumption that you and your reader are already on the same side. Another way is to use **rhetorical questions**. What rhetorical question would convey your attitude and draw in your reader at the same time? An effective example of a rhetorical question here might be 'We've all seen American programmes about famous families, but what do the stars actually do?'

A **pattern of three** would convince your reader by drawing attention to a particular part of your response. You've already decided some celebrities are bad role models. Maybe you could apply this to Premier League footballers. An effective example of a pattern of three here might be 'They're always getting drunk, being chucked out of nightclubs and having affairs'.

Similes and **metaphors** would be effective because they would convince your reader by giving them a point of comparison. Maybe you could apply this to actresses who are known for behaviour that is wild and out of control. An effective metaphor here might be to say that celebrities' lives are 'complete train wrecks'.

Key term

Rhetorical question A question asked to make a point where no answer is expected.

Pattern of three Listing three things to create a specific effect, e.g. 'To pass your exam you need *a pen*, *a piece of paper* and *a brain*'.

Simile A comparison showing the similarity between two quite different things, stating that one is *like* the other, e.g. 'Eating chocolate is *like* going to heaven'.

Metaphor A comparison showing the similarity between two quite different things, stating that one actually *is* the other, e.g. 'When I eat chocolate, I am in heaven'.

Activity 5

1. Using the 'exploring other worlds' ideas that you've already decided on, look again at the language features listed on page 52 and choose three that have not already been used.

   Think of one example of each that could be included in your final response. Think of how to convince your reader and convey your attitude using these language features.

2. Share your ideas with a partner and make a note of any suggestions that could improve your use of selected language features.

Openings

In order to interest your reader immediately, it is essential to write an engaging opening. The opening paragraph, especially the first sentence, is crucial.

In the sample question on page 101 about 'celebrities', you have already decided on the content of your opening paragraph in your plan:

> 1. Introduction – comment on the position of celebrities in society; say you mostly agree with the statement.

Now you need to decide on the most effective way of writing an opening paragraph that starts with an interesting and engaging first sentence and includes your clearly defined point of view, plus any evidence, vocabulary choices or other language features that are relevant at this stage. The example below is annotated to show you how these key skills can be applied. It is taken from a Band 3 response.

> 'Celebrities exploit their position in society and offer nothing in return.' Write an article for a magazine of your choice, arguing for or against this idea.

interesting and engaging first sentence – also comments on the position of celebrities in society

anecdote

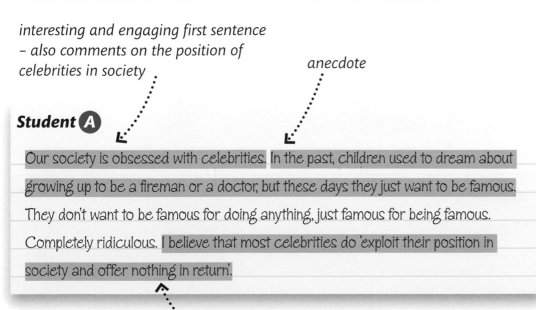

Student A

Our society is obsessed with celebrities. In the past, children used to dream about growing up to be a fireman or a doctor, but these days they just want to be famous. They don't want to be famous for doing anything, just famous for being famous. Completely ridiculous. I believe that most celebrities do 'exploit their position in society and offer nothing in return'.

clearly defined point of view

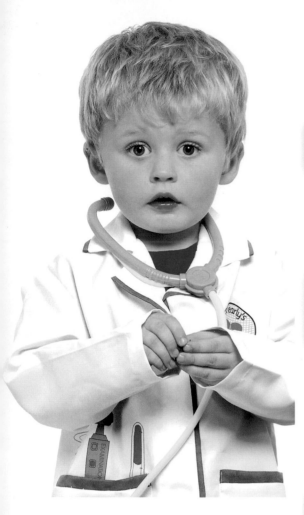

Sentences

Notice the different sentence types that are used in Student A's opening paragraph. Varying your sentence structure is another way to convince your reader. There are four main types of sentence:

1. A simple sentence has a subject and a main verb, for example:

> Our society is obsessed with celebrities.
>
> subject   main verb

2. A compound sentence is where two or more simple sentences are joined together to make one longer sentence, for example:

> In the past, children used to dream about growing up to be a fireman or a doctor, but these days they just want to be famous.
>
> first simple   joining word   second simple
> sentence   sentence

3. A complex sentence is where one part of a sentence is dependent on the other, for example:

> They don't want to be famous for doing anything, just famous for being famous.

The word 'just' leads into the second part of the sentence, which would not make sense without the first part.

4. A minor sentence consists of very few words used deliberately to create an effect, for example:

> Completely ridiculous.

Sentences with one or two words can be effective, but they should not be over-used.

Activity 6

1. Using your 'exploring other worlds' plan and the ideas you've already decided on, write your opening paragraph. Think of a first sentence that will interest and engage your reader immediately, and make sure you vary your sentences.

2. Share your opening paragraph with a partner and make a note of any suggestions that could improve it.

Paragraphs

Paragraphs are important because they help you to organize your ideas and make your response easy to follow. All writing needs an opening paragraph to introduce the topic, a final paragraph to conclude the topic and several paragraphs in between.

Look back over page 87 to remind yourself how to paragraph your response effectively, and then look at the plan on page 103. You will see that a new paragraph is started each time the subject changes. When writing to argue, **discursive markers** like 'however' can be used to link your paragraphs, as well as to link the ideas within your paragraphs.

A complete sample response

Now read the following complete response by Student A. It follows the original plan and is annotated to show you how evidence, vocabulary choices and other language features could be effectively included. This response would be placed at the top of Band 3 as it includes so many of the key skills.

> 'Celebrities exploit their position in society and offer nothing in return.' Write an article for a magazine of your choice, arguing for or against this idea.

interesting and engaging first sentence – also comments on the position of celebrities in society

anecdote

Student A

Our society is obsessed with celebrities. In the past, children used to dream about growing up to be a fireman or a doctor, but these days they just want to be famous. They don't want to be famous for doing anything, just famous for being famous. Completely ridiculous. I believe that most celebrities do 'exploit their position in society and offer nothing in return'.

clearly defined opinion

Notice that the idea about celebrities inspiring us has not been included so that there are not too many reasons in the counter-argument. Plans are there to guide you, but can be adapted at any time.

fact

rhetorical question – involves the reader

example

effective verb

emotive language

pattern of three

metaphor

effective adjective

I suppose there are some good celebrities in society who entertain us. Film stars like Robert Pattinson and Johnny Depp at least have talent and are good looking, and Angelina Jolie does lots of work for charity, as well as adopting children from developing countries. Gary Barlow is another one. He's a brilliant singer, writes great songs, plus he has a beautiful wife and children. He also comes across as genuine. Celebrities like these do offer something to society so in a way I don't agree with the statement.

However, mostly I do think that 'celebrities exploit their position in society and offer nothing in return' because many of them have no talent at all, especially those in TV reality shows. We've all seen American programmes about famous families but what do the stars actually do? Nothing. They're rolling in money to start with and just get paid loads more for being filmed. Sometimes, the children of these families get to do glamorous things like creating their own perfume or presenting the MTV awards, all because they have a father who is extremely rich and once made a TV show. British reality TV stars are the same, just flaunting their fake tans and designer clothes, and making little kids think that's normal. None of them live in the real world like the rest of us.

And don't get me started on premier league footballers! OK, they may have talent but the behaviour of some of them is disgusting. They're always getting drunk, being chucked out of nightclubs and having affairs. I suppose you can't say they 'offer nothing in return' because they're the best players we've got, but they definitely 'exploit their position'. Then you get talented actresses who are complete train wrecks. They make successful Hollywood movies, but the rest of the time they're out of control, getting done for drink driving or possession of drugs, and then checking themselves in and out of rehab. Celebrities like this are worse than the ones who've got no talent at all.

Overall, I agree with the idea that 'celebrities exploit their position in society and offer nothing in return'. Although there are some talented celebrities, most are brainless bimbos or drunks and they're really bad role models for our children. Society would be better off without them.

Try it yourself (with support)

Writing your own complete response

Now you are going to put all the key skills into practice in a complete response to Question 6. You'll be given some support to help you.

Look back over pages 101–112 to remind yourself of how to approach writing to argue.

Activity 7

> Many people believe that it is our duty to support space exploration, whatever the cost. Write an article for a website, which argues for or against the idea of exploring other worlds.

Remember to:

- use your plan
- start with an interesting and engaging first sentence
- start with the opening paragraph you have already written
- include your evidence, effective vocabulary choices and other language features in the appropriate places
- vary your sentences
- use paragraphs correctly.

Exam tips

Remember, how effectively you communicate is the most important skill. If you make too many mistakes in spelling, punctuation and grammar, you will not be able to communicate your ideas to your reader.

Assessing and improving

Look again at the Mark Scheme on pages 72–73. When you have written your response, you need finally to check the accuracy of your work. In the exam, you should allow a few minutes at the end to read through carefully what you have written, checking for any mistakes in spelling, punctuation and grammar.

Activity 8   **Peer-assessment**

1. Now swap your response with a partner. Does your partner's response:

    a. start with an interesting and engaging first sentence?

    b. include evidence, effective vocabulary choices and other language features in appropriate places?

    c. use a varied range of sentences?

    d. use paragraphs correctly?

    e. use spelling, punctuation and grammar accurately? For example, check:

    - spelling – have they confused words that sound the same but are spelt differently, such as 'there/their/they're'?

    - punctuation – have they separated sentences using commas when they should have used full stops?

    - grammar – have they confused singular and plural verbs, such as 'we was' instead of 'we were'?

2. Make some notes on what your partner has done successfully and what could be improved.

3. Now spend a few minutes giving your partner some feedback on their work.

Now read the following complete response by Student B. It follows a similar plan to Student A's and also includes evidence, effective vocabulary choices and other language features. It would be placed in Band 4.

'Celebrities exploit their position in society and offer nothing in return.' Write an article for a magazine of your choice, arguing for or against this idea.

Student B

The cult of celebrity is a huge part of modern society, from businessmen like Richard Branson and Alan Sugar to famous personalities like Simon Cowell and David Beckham. These people are excellent role models because they show us that if you work hard you'll be rewarded. Do they 'exploit their position in society'? I think they probably do, but I don't see any reason why they shouldn't!

Many celebrities are good for society. They entertain, inspire and occasionally educate the rest of us. Some have created ground-breaking inventions that have helped shape modern life and technology as we know it. Some are athletes, like Usain Bolt, who inspire not just one country but the whole world. Some are actors turned politicians and others are politicians turned actors. Each of them affects the world in their own way and they devote their lives to making it a healthier, happier, better place to live. These celebrities are idolized by millions of people. Children want to meet them, men want to be them and women want to marry them. I don't see why they shouldn't 'exploit their position in society'. They worked hard for it.

Of course, there are celebrities who 'offer nothing in return'. Our TVs are littered with reality stars who live their lives being famous for simply being famous. There's no substance to them. They're just plastic and glitter. Programmes like 'The Only Way is Essex' make sure our society is full of wannabes who are prepared to degrade themselves and do anything for a few minutes in the spotlight. These very popular, very wealthy, very stupid people have absolutely no talent and do 'offer nothing in return'.

◀ **Assessing the response**

Band 4: convincing/compelling ✔
Band 3: clarity/success
Band 2: some
Band 1: limited

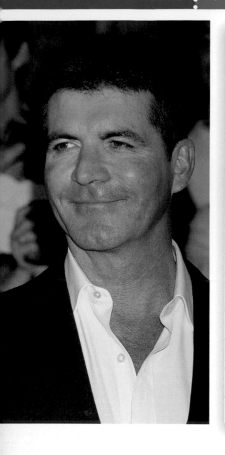

But maybe they deserve our sympathy rather than our disapproval. Beneath the glossy surfaces, many of these celebrities are sad, hollow shells of people. They know their life of glitz and glamour won't last, but they want to hold on to it for as long as they can and they spend their time darting in and out of rehab like scared rabbits. You can't blame them. We treat them like they're something special, which makes them act like they're something special, and their views on the world get twisted. Before 'Heat' and 'OK' sucked them in, I'm sure they used to be happy people with dreams and aspirations just like the rest of us.

And this is why, although there are celebrities who do 'exploit their position in society and offer nothing in return', I don't blame them for it. Many celebrities do have talent and deserve our respect and admiration, and those who don't I just feel sorry for. And I remember that it's not their fault they have become what they are. It's ours.

Activity 9   **Peer-assessment**

In groups of four, re-read the two student responses (pages 111–112 and 115–116) and discuss what Student B does that Student A doesn't. To get you started you could compare:

1. the opening sentences

2. the chosen tone

3. the use of evidence

4. vocabulary choices

5. the use of other language features

6. sentence variety

7. paragraphs. For example, in Student A's response:

- the second paragraph that starts 'I suppose there are some good celebrities in society who entertain us' lets the reader know that the positive qualities of celebrities are going to be considered within that paragraph.

Section 2: Writing to persuade

In some ways, writing to persuade is very similar to writing to argue. They both involve convincing someone and the way to approach the question in the exam is identical. However, the key skills that you need to demonstrate in your response have a slightly different emphasis.

To begin with, remind yourself how to approach the question by referring back to pages 101–116.

Activity 10

1. Copy out the sample question below and identify its purpose, audience and form.

> The goal of the London 2012 Olympics was to 'inspire a generation'. Write a letter to the Prime Minister, persuading him to fund projects that inspire young people to take up sport.

2. Draw a spider diagram with 'ways to inspire young people to take up sport' in the centre and write your ideas around this. One way might be to increase the number of PE lessons in the school curriculum.

3. Select the two or three ideas you think you can write about most effectively.

4. Write a plan that starts with an introduction, ends with a conclusion and includes your chosen two or three ways of inspiring young people to take up sport.

5. Decide on the tone you want to adopt.

6. Discuss your plan with a partner and share your ideas. Make a note of any suggestions that improve your plan.

Exam tips

If you are asked to write a letter in the exam, do not include an address but begin with 'Dear ... ' and sign off appropriately. If you begin 'Dear Madam' or 'Dear Sir', end with 'Yours faithfully'. If you begin with a person's name, for example, 'Dear Mr Cameron', end with 'Yours sincerely'.

Practising the key skills

To persuade means to convince someone to do or think something. The best way to convince your reader when writing to persuade is by making them believe they will be better off if they do or think as you suggest. This is achieved both by the tone you choose and by your choice of language.

Read Student A's complete response below. This response would be placed at the top of Band 3 as it includes so many of the key skills.

> The goal of the London 2012 Olympics was to 'inspire a generation'. Write a letter to the Prime Minister, persuading him to fund projects that inspire young people to take up sport.

Assessing the response ▶

Band 4: convincing/compelling	
Band 3: clarity/success	✔
Band 2: some	
Band 1: limited	

Student Ⓐ

Dear Sir,

What Team GB did at the London 2012 Olympics was amazing. We won more gold medals than we've ever won before and it's really important that we do the same or better at the next Olympics in Rio. They said the goal was to 'inspire a generation', which means we must find possible athletes while they are still young and train them to become the best in the world. I'm therefore writing to you today to persuade you to fund projects that inspire young people to take up sport.

We all know that one way to make sure we have successful athletes in the future is to encourage them to do sport in schools, but the only way we can do this is if schools are properly funded. I really like gymnastics but the equipment in our school is well past its sell-by date. I was lucky enough to get tickets to see Beth Tweddle win her bronze medal and she was fantastic. It's obvious that people like me will never be as good as that unless schools have enough money to train us in modern, well-equipped, state-of-the art facilities. I know there is a recession on at the moment and nobody has any money but you have to find it from somewhere if you want young people to fulfil their potential. You don't want the talents of our British youth going to waste, do you?

The other area where money is needed is in local communities where there have to be more sports clubs and teams. Not all young people hang around in gangs or spend their lives glued to their Xbox or computer screen. Some of us would love to try out different sports and become the next Jessica Ennis, but a recent survey discovered that 47% of young people trying to get into sport don't have any nearby facilities. We must provide opportunities for them to join clubs and teams so that they develop a competitive spirit. Maybe local businesses would be willing to contribute some money if it was you, personally, who asked them? Please help us, Prime Minister.

I know you are a very busy man and I would like to thank you for taking the time to read my letter. I've only written because I think this is a really important issue. If the goal of the London 2012 Olympics was to 'inspire a generation' then it worked, but we need money to make it happen. Please will you consider funding the projects I've suggested so that more young people are inspired to take up sport? After all, we need to find our gold medallists of the future.

Yours faithfully,

Exam tips

Notice that the argument and counter-argument have been combined throughout the response so that any objections to the proposals are considered (with possible solutions) and dismissed at the same time. This is an alternative way to structure your response when writing to argue or persuade.

Key term

Imperative A command or instruction, for example, 'you have to find it'.

Activity 11

Once you have read Student A's response, re-read 'Selecting language' on page 51.

1. Look at the sentence that begins 'It's obvious that people like me will never be as good as that...'. This is an example of an opinion presented as a fact and suggests there is no room for disagreement.

   a. Find three examples in the response on pages 118–119 where **imperatives** have been used to present an opinion as a fact.
   b. Why is it effective to use imperatives when writing to persuade?

2. Look at the types of evidence that have been included in the response.

   a. Identify one anecdote, two examples and one statistic.
   b. Why is it effective to use them when writing to persuade?

3. Look at the sentence that begins 'We all know that one way to make sure we have successful athletes ...'. This is an example of direct address.

   a. Find three examples where 'you' is used to address the reader.
   b. Why is it effective to use 'we' or 'you' when writing to persuade?

4. Questions have also been used to address the reader directly.

   a. Find one example of a straightforward question and two examples of rhetorical questions in Student A's response.
   b. Why is it effective to use questions when writing to persuade?

5. Identify other language features used in Student A's response and explain why they are effective when writing to persuade.

6. Discuss your answers with a partner and share your ideas.

7. With your partner, compare the use of language features when writing to persuade with how they are used when writing to argue. What are the similarities and differences?

Now read Student B's complete response opposite. It follows the same plan as Student A and includes similar language features. It would be placed in Band 4.

Activity 12

In groups of four, discuss what Student B does that Student A doesn't. To get you started, you could compare:

1. the first and final sentences
2. the chosen tone
3. the use of language features
4. the use of paragraphs
5. the variety of sentences.

The goal of the London 2012 Olympics was to 'inspire a generation'. Write a letter to the Prime Minister, persuading him to fund projects that inspire young people to take up sport.

Student B

Band 4: convincing/compelling ✔

Band 3: clarity/success

Band 2: some

Band 1: limited

Dear Mr Cameron,

The London 2012 Olympics was the best for Great Britain in over 100 years, mainly due to the time and money spent on honing the skills and techniques of our athletes, taking them from mere contenders to gold medal winners. Now we have to capitalize on this achievement and create a sporting legacy for the young people of Great Britain. Our athletes were only able to achieve such incredible success because they had people who believed in them. The purpose of this letter is to persuade you to believe in me.

I have been truly inspired to embody the motto of the Games: to become faster, higher, stronger. As a sprinter, the heroics of double Olympic gold medallist Mo Farah and triple Olympic Champion Usain Bolt overwhelmed me. It also made me determined to succeed, but this can only happen with your support. Sports facilities need to be funded in schools. Students must have free access to specialized equipment and coaching programmes, and this can only happen if schools have enough money. I appreciate that we are in the middle of an economic crisis but the mandate of the Games was to 'inspire a generation' and it is therefore essential that you increase the funding to schools so that every student has the opportunity to realize their potential.

Sports programmes in the community are also necessary. It is where athletes are made. You may think that the youth of today are too busy hanging round on street corners or sitting in front of their computer screens or even that they are just not interested, but they are. During the Games, thousands fled to the capital to support the Brownlee brothers on their quest to Olympic glory and thousands more watched with mouths agape as Sir Chris Hoy hauled in his sixth gold. The country is enthusiastic about sport and, more importantly, the youth are enthusiastic about sport. I know I'm asking for more money but maybe you could get sponsorship from large businesses to help. All I know is that sports programmes in the community are important to motivate and encourage the competitive spirit within all young athletes.

If you agree to fund these projects, the main thing that will happen is that a new generation will learn to believe. Because the real problem, Prime Minister, is not the money or the logistics of producing these facilities but the ability to instil belief in our youth. Our Olympic heroes have done their part to 'inspire a generation', but the time has come for the baton to be passed on. I hope I am successful in persuading you to believe in us because if you don't, who will?

Yours sincerely,

Try it yourself (with support)

Writing your own complete response

Now you are going to put all the key skills into practice in a complete response to another Question 6 task.

Look back over pages 117–121 to remind yourself of how to approach writing to persuade.

Activity 13

1. 'Why would anyone want to become a teacher when young people have no respect for authority these days?' Write an article for a careers magazine, persuading readers that teaching is a worthwhile profession.

2. Check your response and correct any mistakes in spelling, punctuation and grammar.

So far, you have learnt how to approach Question 6 by focusing on two things:

- what to do before you start to write your response
- what key skills to include in your response.

Now see how confident you feel that you have understood this approach by completing the self-assessment opposite.

Self-assessment

1.	I have learnt that the topic I have to write about is given to me in the question and I need to identify the purpose, audience and form.	Not sure	Confident
2.	I have learnt that before I start to write my response, I need to think of ideas and then write a plan.	Not sure	Confident
3.	I have learnt that I need to think about tone before I start to write my response.	Not sure	Confident
4.	I have learnt that how effectively I communicate is the most important skill.	Not sure	Confident
5.	I have learnt that when writing to argue, I need to include evidence, effective vocabulary choices and other relevant language features.	Not sure	Confident
6.	I have learnt that when writing to persuade, I need to emphasize slightly different language features from when writing to argue.	Not sure	Confident
7.	I have learnt that I need to start with an effective opening and that my first sentence is crucial.	Not sure	Confident
8.	I have learnt that I need to vary my sentence structure.	Not sure	Confident
9.	I have learnt that I need to organize my response into paragraphs and link them effectively.	Not sure	Confident
10.	I have learnt that I need to check the accuracy of my work for spelling, punctuation and grammar mistakes when I finish writing.	Not sure	Confident

Try it yourself (on your own)

Write a complete response to each of the following tasks:

'So many marriages end in divorce that it's pointless getting married in the first place.' Write an article for a woman's magazine arguing for, or against, marriage.

'The world would be a more peaceful place if all the world's leaders were women.' Write an article for an online magazine, persuading readers that women, or men, make better leaders.

Section A: Reading

Read Source 1, 'The flame that will never go out' by Oliver Holt.

1. What do you understand from the article about how attitudes towards the Paralympics have changed?
    (8 marks)

Now read Source 2, the article and the picture that goes with it called 'Underwater Wheelchair Freewheels the Deep' by Nic Halverson.

2. Explain how the headline and picture are effective and how they link with the text.
    (8 marks)

Now read Source 3, *Reading Blind* by Stephen Kuusisto, which is an extract from a non-fiction book.

3. Explain some of the thoughts and feelings Stephen has while attending school.
    (8 marks)

Now you need to refer to Source 3, *Reading Blind*, and either Source 1 or Source 2.

4. You are going to compare two texts, one of which you have chosen. Compare the ways in which language is used for effect in the two texts. Give some examples and analyse what the effects are.
    (16 marks)

Section B: Writing

5. Write a letter to your local councillor, informing him of the lack of disabled facilities in your area and explaining how you think they should be improved.

6. 'People who are disabled in any way should be educated separately because they will never cope in normal schools.' Write an online article that argues for or against the integration of disabled children into mainstream education.

Source 1

The flame that will never go out

ONCE, NOT VERY LONG AGO, the Paralympics was an event that could not stand alone. It was an add-on to the Olympics. It was an obligation. Some said it was the price you paid for staging the Greatest Show on Earth. Others muttered that the event was a gesture to political correctness, a deformed limb, superfluous and awkward.

It seems strange now. It seems prehistoric. Because what has happened in the last 11 days in London has changed the world. Not for everyone. Not for those who were already enlightened. Not for those who have, for their own reasons, remained unmoved. But for many, the world has altered. For the better. The move towards inclusivity and away from discrimination against the disabled has accelerated.

When the athletes who have graced these Paralympics made their way into the Olympic Stadium for the closing ceremony, many among them had become our heroes. Once we might have looked at disabled athletes and seen a tragedy. Now we look and see triumph. Now we look and see people not to be pitied but to be admired. Now we do not avert our gaze. Instead we stare in wonder.

'Is this a kind of magic?' Freddie Mercury's voice sang to the stadium as the last of the athletes joined the party.

And the answer is, 'Yes, it is.' Pity has been banished. It has been replaced by something closer to envy.

It was only a couple of months ago that Oscar Pistorius, the great South African runner, felt the need to warn against displays of pity masquerading as shows of support at the Paralympics. Last Thursday night, Pistorius's T44 men's 100m race against Britain's Jonnie Peacock drew 6.6 million viewers on Channel 4. Those who tuned in to watch Peacock and Pistorius did not tune in out of pity or mawkishness. They wanted to watch a race. They wanted to watch a showdown between the biggest name in Paralympic sport and a new idol.

Ellie Simmonds was there, too. The S6 swimmer has become one of the most popular sportswomen in the country and won two golds, a silver and bronze here. She has become a byword for indomitability, too. But also for humility. And willpower.

When the time came finally to extinguish the flame that has burned in London, it seemed fitting that Peacock and Simmonds, two of those who have made it burn brightest, should be involved in the honour. The flame has been the symbol of an enchanted summer. The things we have witnessed here these last 11 days, the changes the events have engendered, means that it will never really go out.

Source 2

Underwater Wheelchair Freewheels the Deep

When it comes to diving into the waters of self expression, British artist Sue Austin is as freewheeling as they come. As the 2012 Paralympics kick off this week in London, Austin has been making waves with a series of performances and film screenings of 'Creating the Spectacle,' a theatrical video of Austin as she navigates the deep in her underwater wheelchair.

Austin, who's been in a wheelchair since 1996, told the BBC that she first had the idea for the project after learning to scuba dive in 2005.

'When we started talking to people about it, engineers were saying it wouldn't work, the wheelchair would go into a spin, it was not designed to go through water – but I was sure it would,' she said.

Austin's wheelchair is powered by two dive propulsion thrusters under her seat. To steer, Austin slips her feet into an acrylic, U-shaped fin reminiscent of stingray wings. She also uses floatation devices for buoyancy.

Austin modified a standard-issue wheelchair from Britain's National Health Service (NHS) because it 'is one of the most ubiquitous images of disability' and she wants this project to leave 'a legacy of attitudinal change' in regards to the public perception of disability.

The wheelchair has patents pending and is already making a splash outside of the art world.

'We've had Professional Association of Diving Instructors course directors and very experienced divers saying they would pay to hire it,' Austin said.

'The Oceanography department at the University of Plymouth, where I did a BA in performing art, said it would make their courses accessible to students with disabilities.'

Source 3

Although Stephen has limited vision in one eye, he is registered blind, and recalls how hard it was to cope when attending a mainstream school in America in the early 1960s.

Reading Blind

In school, the printed word scurries away from my one 'reading eye' – words, in fact, seem to me like insects released from a box. While the class reads aloud, I watch the spirals of hypnotic light that ripple across my eyes when I move them from side to side. I do not belong here. My little body at this desk is something uncanny – a thing that belongs in the darkness and that has been brought to daylight.

But I talk, answer questions, make others laugh. I'm interested in everything and tell the class that I can spell Tchaikovsky.

Mrs Edinger becomes the first saint in my life. She takes it upon herself to help me read. After school we sit at her desk, and with my nose jammed into the pages, we go over the words. And though I'm squinting and struggling supremely over each alphabetic squiggle, she has the patience of an archaeologist, one who dusts the microscopic shards before putting them away. With her, I hold my eye very still and make out the words.

Years later I learn from my mother that Mrs Edinger is a black woman and perhaps the first person of African American heritage to teach in this local New Hampshire school. We are mutual explorers as we go over the hopeless print. She's noticed my determination and has figured out that I have a photographic memory. This probably contributes to her desire to see me read – she knows I'll retain the words that I've struggled so hard to grasp.

Hours of after-school time are spent before I can match the class in reading. I have to hold my book an inch from my eye. The exhaustion of this is like the deep fatigue drivers feel after being too long on the road. The ordinary effort of reading is, for me, a whole-body experience. My neck, shoulders, and, finally, my lower back contract with pain. The legally blind know what it is to be old: even before the third grade I am hunched and shaking with effort, always on the verge of tears, seeing by approximation, craving a solid sentence. Then the words dissolve or run like ants. Nevertheless I find a lighted room inside my head. I am not blind. I am not the target of pranks.

But leaving my reading lesson, a boy I think of as a friend steals my glasses and my panic brings me alive like a tree filled with birds: I navigate with my hands.

'Hey, Blindo, over here!'

He laughs along with several others, then they run.

I lunge with my arms straight following the sounds of sneakers. I'm determined not to cry: steel keys revolve and lock in my brain. Then I trip on a curb and cut my hand on a drain.

To this day I picture that boy clutching my glasses at a safe distance and watching me drift about. I learned early that with my glasses I'm blind, without them I'm a wild white face, a body groping, the miner who's come suddenly into the light.

On this particular afternoon I am instantly put on display. More than thirty years have passed since that moment, but I'm still disconcerted by what it felt like to belong so thoroughly to another person, to be, in effect, their possession.

OXFORD
UNIVERSITY PRESS

Great Clarendon Street, Oxford OX2 6DP

Oxford University Press is a department of the University of Oxford.
It furthers the University's objective of excellence in research,
scholarship, and education by publishing worldwide in

Oxford New York

Auckland Cape Town Dar es Salaam Hong Kong Karachi
Kuala Lumpur Madrid Melbourne Mexico City Nairobi
New Delhi Shanghai Taipei Toronto

With offices in

Argentina Austria Brazil Chile Czech Republic France Greece
Guatemala Hungary Italy Japan South Korea Poland Portugal
Singapore Switzerland Thailand Turkey Ukraine Vietnam

Oxford is a registered trade mark of Oxford University Press in the UK
and in certain other countries

© Oxford University Press 2013

Database right Oxford University Press (maker)

First published 2013

British Library Cataloguing in Publication Data

Data available

ISBN 978-019-839039-8

10 9 8 7 6 5 4 3

Printed in China by Printplus

Acknowledgements

The publisher and author would like to thank the following for their
permission to reproduce photographs and other copyright material:

Cover, p2, p4, p70: FAUP/Shutterstock; **p7:** leungchopan/Shutterstock; **p8:** kurhan/Shutterstock; **p9:** Robert Kneschke/Shutterstock; **p13:** Eric Isselee/Shutterstock; **p15:** kldy/Shutterstock; **p16:** Jay Williams/Telegraph Media Group Limited 2012; **p20&21:** pio3/Shutterstock; **p22&23:** Allan Bell/Alamy; **p24:** Peter Byrne/PA Archive/Press Association Images; **p25&28:** OUP; **p29&30:** Bloomberg via Getty Images; **p35:** Kerstin Joensson/AP/Press Association Images; **p37-39:** NASA; **p41:** Natursports/Shutterstock; **p43:** Geanina Bechea/Shutterstock; **p45:** Galyna Andrushko/Shutterstock; **p47:** AP/AP/Press Association Images; **p48:** s_bukley/Shutterstock.com; **p51:** Yuri Arcurs/Shutterstock; **p51:** (cutout): Ingvar Bjork/Shutterstock; **p53:** Robert Kneschke/Shutterstock; **p54:** Andrey Shadrin/Shutterstock; **p55:** Eric Isselee/Shutterstock; **p57:** Marci Paravia/Shutterstock; **p58:** Robert Kneschke/Shutterstock; **p58-59:** Natursports/Shutterstock; **p61:** Colin Monteath/ Hedgehog House/Minden Pictures/Corbis; **p62:** Bloomberg via Getty Images; **p63:** Jimmy Chin/Aurora Photos/Corbis; **p65:** Vadim Petrakov/Shutterstock; **p66:** charles taylor/Shutterstock; **p68:** Kerstin Joensson/AP/Press Association Images; **p75:** Andrey Arkusha/Shutterstock; **p76:** Everett Collection/Shutterstock; **p78l:** Juriah Mosin/Shutterstock; **p78r:** Nadina/Shutterstock; **p78b:** JJ pixs/Shutterstock; **p79:** Suzanne Tucker/Shutterstock; **p80:** Fer Gregory/Shutterstock; **p81:** Vlue/Shutterstock; **p82:** jwblinn/Shutterstock; **p83:** Sakala/Shutterstock; **p84:** ARENA Creative/Shutterstock; **p89:** Monkey Business Images/Shutterstock; **p90l:** oliveromg/Shutterstock; **p90r:** Stanislav Komogorov/Shutterstock; **p93l&m:** wet nose/Shutterstock; **p93r:** Cienpies Design/Shutterstock; **p93b:** piotr_pabijan/Shutterstock; **p94:** Yuri Arcurs/Shutterstock; **p94-95:** Ayelet Keshet/Shutterstock; **p97:** Andresr/Shutterstock; **p98:** sint/Shutterstock; **p101:** Yuri Arcurs/Shutterstock; **p102:** FotograFFF/Shutterstock; **p103:** Yuri Arcurs/Shutterstock; **p105:** mozzyb/Shutterstock; **p106:** Nabil Mounzer/epa/Corbis; **p108:** mironov/Shutterstock; **p110:** Daniel Gale/Shutterstock; **p113:** Triff/Shutterstock; **p116:** Pictorial Press Ltd/Alamy; **p117:** ALLSTAR Picture Library/Alamy; **p118:** ArtThailand/Shutterstock; **p120:** PCN Photography/Alamy; **p122:** Monkey Business Images/Shutterstock; **p126:** Freewheeling/Norman Lomax/Rex Features

The publisher and author are grateful for permission to reprint extracts
from the following copyright material:

Buzz Aldrin with Ken Abraham: *Magnificent Desolation: the long journey home from the moon* (Bloomsbury, 2009), reprinted by permission of the publisher.

Harriet Cooke: 'IQ Tests: Women score higher than men', *Sunday Telegraph*, 15.7.2012, copyright © Telegraph Media Group Ltd 2012, reprinted by permission of TMG.

Peter Cripps: 'Crawling crabs sidle into UK to pinch festive sales', *The Independent*, 30.11.2011, copyright © The Independent 2011, reprinted by permission of Independent Print Ltd.

Wang Dajun translated by Roddy Flagg: 'Panda breeding success ignores their disappearing habitat', from www.chinadialogue.net and as published in *The Guardian*, 6.3.2012, reprinted by permission of China Dialogue Trust Ltd.

James Day & **Oliver Stallwood:** 'Rise of the Robots: Machines capable of replacing human workforce', *Metro*, 6.12.2011, reprinted by permission of Solo Syndication for Associated Newspapers Ltd.

Sally Emerson: 'Dumbo in the Jungle', *The Sunday Times*, 5.2.2012, copyright © Sally Emerson 2012, reprinted by permission of the author.

Stephen Fry: *Stephen Fry in America* (HarperCollins, 2008), copyright © Stephen Fry 2008, reprinted by permission of HarperCollins Publishers Ltd.

Richard Gray: 'Facebook Generation suffer information withdrawal syndrome', *Sunday Telegraph*, 2.1.2011, copyright © Telegraph Media Group Ltd 2011, reprinted by permission of TMG.

Nic Halverson: 'Underwater wheelchair freewheels the deep', *Discovery News*, 29.8.2012, reprinted by permission of Discovery Communications, LLC.

Oliver Holt: 'The flame that will never go out: How the Paralympics festival of sport has changed the world in 11 days', *Sunday Mirror*, 9.9.2012, copyright © Mirrorpix, reprinted by permission of Mirror Syndication International.

Stephen Kuusisto: *Planet of the Blind* (Faber, 1998), reprinted by permission of the publishers, Faber & Faber Ltd.

Robert Macfarlane: *Mountains of the Mind: a History of Fascination* (Granta, 2003), reprinted by permission of Granta Books.

Linda Serck: 'The problem with gifted children', BBC Berkshire News, 13.10.2009, reprinted by permission of BBC News.

Clover Stroud: 'Dogs in the classroom: reading with a fluffy friend ', *Daily Telegraph*, 3.7.2012, copyright © Telegraph Media Group Ltd 2012, reprinted by permission of TMG.

David Taylor: 'Full steam ahead for railway plans', headline from *Hull Daily Mail*, 31.5.2012, reprinted by permission of Mail News and Media.

Simon Turnbull: 'Ennis weighs in with telling response to "fat" critics', *The Independent*, 28.5.2012, copyright © The Independent 2012, reprinted by permission of Independent Print Ltd.

Although we have made every effort to trace and contact all copyright
holders before publication this has not been possible in all cases. If notified,
the publisher will rectify any errors or omissions at the earliest opportunity.

Author acknowledgements

I would like to thank Santa's Little Helpers, Ramender Crompton for
encouraging them and Chris Bowden for the Jackanory sessions.